LOVE'S LABOUR

ALSO BY STEPHEN GROSZ

The Examined Life

LOVE'S LABOUR

STEPHEN GROSZ

Chatto & Windus
London

1 3 5 7 9 10 8 6 4 2

Chatto & Windus, an imprint of Vintage, is part of the
Penguin Random House group of companies

Vintage, Penguin Random House UK, One Embassy Gardens,
8 Viaduct Gardens, London SW11 7BW

penguin.co.uk/vintage
global.penguinrandomhouse.com

First published by Chatto & Windus in 2025

Copyright © Stephen Grosz 2025

The moral right of the author has been asserted

Penguin Random House values and supports copyright. Copyright fuels creativity, encourages diverse voices, promotes freedom of expression and supports a vibrant culture. Thank you for purchasing an authorised edition of this book and for respecting intellectual property laws by not reproducing, scanning or distributing any part of it by any means without permission. You are supporting authors and enabling Penguin Random House to continue to publish books for everyone. No part of this book may be used or reproduced in any manner for the purpose of training artificial intelligence technologies or systems. In accordance with Article 4(3) of the DSM Directive 2019/790, Penguin Random House expressly reserves this work from the text and data mining exception.

Typeset in 10/18pt MillerText by Six Red Marbles UK, Thetford, Norfolk
Printed and bound in Great Britain by Clays Ltd, Elcograf S.p.A.

The authorised representative in the EEA is Penguin Random House Ireland,
Morrison Chambers, 32 Nassau Street, Dublin D02 YH68

A CIP catalogue record for this book is available from the British Library

HB ISBN 9780701188962
TPB ISBN 9780701188979

Penguin Random House is committed to a sustainable future
for our business, our readers and our planet. This book is made
from Forest Stewardship Council® certified paper.

To my family, with love

For one person to love another: that is perhaps the most difficult of all our tasks, the work for which all other work is but preparation.

                                      RAINER MARIA RILKE,
                                          LETTERS TO A YOUNG POET

Remember that all our failures are ultimately failures in love.

                                      IRIS MURDOCH, *THE BELL*

Contents

Prologue: Surrender	1
Marry Me	7
Lost Love	31
An Impossible Desire	49
Carnal Knowledge: Three Cases	77
Connections	93
The Gift	117
Sparks	123
Love and Time	131
Going Home	141
Hauntings	147
Epilogue: Love and Happiness	173
SOURCES AND NOTES	177
ACKNOWLEDGEMENTS	187

Prologue: Surrender

It is January 1983, the first Monday after New Year's. Dark skies; pounding, icy rain. Harley Street is filled with taxis. When the traffic lights change, the taxis don't move. There is nowhere for them to go. Umbrellas bob at odd angles, their users tilting to avoid collisions.

I find 5 Upper Wimpole Street and ring the bell. The receptionist shows me into a waiting room lit by several standing lamps. There is a coal fire in the fireplace. Dark floorboards, a large rug. I sit at the far side of the room so I can watch the door.

To become a psychoanalyst, you must have an analysis yourself, and this training analysis will have a profound effect on the way you do the work – how could it be otherwise? I am waiting to begin my first psychoanalytic session.

At exactly 9 a.m., Dr Limentani appears. He gives a small smile and nods. He shows me into a modest room even warmer than the waiting room, and sits down in his chair behind the psychoanalytic couch.

'Make yourself comfortable. There's the chair or the couch.' He pauses. 'I think the couch is more comfortable.'

Looking back forty years to the start of my life as a psychoanalyst, I remember the shift from outside noise to quiet, from cold to warm. I also remember who I was.

I was thirty-one years old and immature. I was impulsive and quick to fall in love, and often confused intensity with intimacy. I thought I was clear-eyed, but I saw love through the limited and limiting storylines of popular culture. I talked to my friends as if love was a position best filled by a committee. I believed that if I could just find the 'right' person, happiness would automatically follow.

There was so much I didn't understand. I didn't understand that each of us is responsible for our own happiness. That if I didn't treat myself with consideration and care, chances are a good many others wouldn't treat me that way either.

I didn't understand pain. I thought the many kinds of pain we suffer when we love another person – longing, anxiety, grief – were feelings to avoid, symptoms to be removed. I didn't understand that pain is the finest instrument we possess for knowing what we desire.

We deceive ourselves about love – the who, what and why. But we also have the power to undo self-deception. Love's labour is the work we must do to see clearly ourselves and our loved ones. It is our attempt to join the world as it is. 'Love,' Iris Murdoch writes, 'is the perception of individuals. Love is the extremely difficult realisation that something other than oneself is real.' She goes on: 'Love is the discovery of reality.'

My first lesson in love: a distinction between surrender and submission.

I lay down on Dr Limentani's couch and was surprised by my own tears. For most of the first session, I could hardly speak. I think now that this was a response (one which I have since observed in my own patients) to the relief of knowing that someone was there to listen to me, and that he would be there the next day and the day after that, for as long as I wanted to come.

When I did find my voice – a few days later – I spoke to my psychoanalyst about my Oedipus complex, my projections and introjections; my transference and his counter-transference. I gave him my take on Freud and Lacan, Klein and Winnicott. I told him what I thought about recent articles in the *Journal of the American Psychoanalytic Association* and the *International Journal of Psychoanalysis*. He let me carry on in this way for some time, until finally, a few weeks in, he asked, 'Have you noticed that you talk more about psychoanalytic theory than I do?'

What was he suggesting? 'Isn't it in the *Introductory Lectures* that Freud says clinical practice is built upon psychoanalytic theory?' I asked.

'Well, we *could* talk about psychoanalytic theory,' he said. 'But where does that leave *you*?' And, on another occasion: 'Why do you always come to your sessions accompanied by Freud, or one of the greats of psychoanalysis? Why are you so frightened to be here on your own?'

At the time I thought that Dr Limentani was suggesting that, by embracing psychoanalytic theory, I was dating the wrong girl, that I should be hanging with *clinical* psychoanalysis, the experience itself. As it turns out, Dr Limentani was beginning to untangle something that was so much a part of me I couldn't see it.

In addition to my fussy expounding on psychoanalytic theory, I was incredibly – maybe compulsively – obedient as a patient: I was never late, never missed a session, paid my bill the day I received it. Dr Limentani saw my desire to please him, to do everything I thought he wanted me to do. Over time, in a series of clear, piercing interpretations, he pointed out to me that I believed that if I *submitted* to him – if I became the patient I imagined he wanted me to be – he would accept me, and this acceptance would lift me, heal me, return me to my life.

I was approaching Dr Limentani just as I had approached so many other people who were important to me. I wanted him to take a shine to me, in the hope that his acceptance – his love – would change me. Through his interpretations, I came to see that this was more than an underlying pattern in my life: it was my life.

It became clear to me that there is a vital distinction to be made between surrendering to something (or someone) and submitting to it. This distinction is something that could have saved

PROLOGUE: SURRENDER

me some suffering if I'd considered it sooner. To surrender is to let go, to experience a release. When two people surrender to each other, they feel alive, empowered, accepted. They feel love.

Submission, or submissiveness, is different. It too begins with a longing to be loved – and yet, submitting to another person leaves us feeling like we've fallen under their control. Submission is transactional: I'll give you what you want – *be* what you want – in return, you will love me. Because this deal is unrealisable, it's doomed, and submission is usually accompanied by feelings of resignation or depression.

Eventually, when I was able to trust Dr Limentani and to leave all of my theorising outside – to surrender to the analysis – I found that I did not often break down in tears. (I also found that the world didn't come to an end when I did cry.) I had other things to say. I don't remember my precise words and his responses; I must have spoken about what was going on in my life – breaking up with a girlfriend, my feelings about my research and training, my mother's cancer. With his quiet insistence on hearing my feelings, dreams and associations, Dr Limentani brought me into the slow work of drawing a map of my internal world. Here is desire; here is envy; here, in this place, is sadness.

Gradually the communication between my internal and external worlds improved – and I experienced this as a release. I found I was better able to make sense of things that once had been mysterious. More than that, I felt less lonely, no longer up against a wall.

I began my psychoanalysis with the belief that, from the start, Dr Limentani knew what I was all about – that to be a psychoanalyst is to know already. The very opposite is true: psychoanalysis is a particular form of not knowing. Psychoanalysis is two people not knowing together. The process of psychoanalysis is to think together, find meaning together. The only way he could get to know me – that *we* could get to know me – was through talking and listening.

Marry Me

1

Looking now at my Filofax from 1989, I see that I had planned to spend the last Saturday in November in Cambridge, at Kettle's Yard. I wanted to see an exhibition of paintings. That plan was scrapped when, late Friday night, I got a call from Sophie A.

Sophie had been given my number by a friend and felt she needed to talk to someone urgently. She and her fiancé, Nicholas – Nick – had spent the previous weekend addressing their wedding invitations. On Monday morning, he'd taken his half of the invitations and posted them. The sixty invitations that Sophie was responsible for were still at her office, in a carrier bag under her desk. She couldn't bring herself to post them, or to bring them home, or to tell Nick about any of it. She wasn't sure what to do. She wasn't even sure she should be ringing me. I offered her a consultation for the next day.

On Saturday, Sophie didn't appear for her appointment. After fifteen minutes, I assumed that she had finally sent the invitations, or had talked to her fiancé and was now living through the consequences. I was in the small kitchen next to my consulting room, making a cup of coffee and opening the post, when my doorbell rang.

The woman on my doorstep was tall and stylish. Her straight dark hair was cut in a geometric chin-length bob. She wore wire-rimmed glasses. With the exception of her jeans, everything she had on was black. She stepped with some hesitancy into the consulting room. Without taking off her coat, Sophie sat down on the edge of the chair opposite me and apologised several times for being late. She explained that she'd stopped off at her parents' house. She had wanted to tell them about the invitations, but, once there, she hadn't been able to.

'I'm probably frightened of their reaction,' she said. 'They really like Nick.' She apologised to me again. She wasn't herself, she said. She worked as an arts correspondent for a national newspaper. She was a responsible person, not indecisive or impulsive.

'Has anything like this ever happened to you before?' I asked.

'Never,' she said.

She told me about her relationship with Nick. They had met through friends, made it through an early wobble when she thought he might still be interested in an old girlfriend. They had always had good sexual chemistry. Of course, there were things that bothered her. He had just been hired as a history lecturer at a London university, and she thought he worked too much. They had the usual squabbles about the dishes and housework. He was still a bit of an adolescent, but weren't all men?

'I can't be easy to live with,' she said. 'I expect him to be as well organised as I am. If I send him to the supermarket for ten things and he comes back with eight of them, it's hard for me to hide my frustration. My "should have done it myself" face.'

But Nick didn't get upset with her about this sort of thing, she said. Other boyfriends had. She sat forward in her chair. She unbuttoned her coat and pushed it back off her shoulders. 'Mr Grosz, I do love Nick. I don't want anyone else. I just don't know what's happening to me. I feel afraid.'

Sophie had grown up in Notting Hill, near the Portobello Road, where her parents owned an antiques business. They did architectural salvage – chimneypieces, door furniture, floors, garden ornaments, lighting, mirrors, textiles and carpets. She felt absolutely terrible that she hadn't been able to tell them about the wedding invitations. She usually told her parents everything. She was an only child, and very close to her parents.

I asked Sophie about her eating and sleeping. She said she'd been waking up early, feeling anxious, and having terrible dreams. The night before had been awful. Fearful that she was going to miss our appointment, she'd woken up again and again to check her alarm clock. At some point, near morning, she fell into a deep sleep and had a dream.

'I dreamed I was in a changing room with my mum and dad. We were all supposed to undress and go through to the showers. Somehow, I realised that we were going to be gassed. There was nothing I could do. We couldn't stay in the changing room. We had to go forward, through the door. We were all going to die.' She looked at me. 'And then I woke up.'

'Why would I dream something like that?' she asked me.

My silence seemed to make Sophie uncomfortable.

She hesitated, then she told me that she wasn't Jewish, Nick wasn't either. This subject – the Holocaust – was not something she'd been thinking about. A few months back, just after Primo Levi died, she'd seen a documentary on television about him, and she'd read one of his books, but that was a while ago. Her dream made no sense to her. We sat facing each other in silence.

After a minute or two, I asked her what she'd been thinking.

She twisted her engagement ring, told me she was embarrassed, and hoped that I wouldn't take it the wrong way, but when her friend had suggested that she come and see me, she'd had the thought that I might be Jewish. Grosz is a Jewish name, isn't it? She'd thought about Freud. He was Jewish. Sophie stopped. 'I sound terrible. I don't know why I dreamed about the Holocaust.'

My intuition was that Sophie's dream wasn't about concentration camps, the Holocaust or Jewishness – her anxiety suggested some anticipated, internal calamity. And yet, although she was offering her associations honestly, freely, and although the dream itself seemed simple, I had to admit, I was struggling to find a way into it. I felt stuck.

I remembered a passage in Freud – if he couldn't disentangle a patient's dream, he would ask the patient to repeat it. Ordinarily, the patient would slightly alter the account – according to Freud, those parts of the dream described differently were revealed as the 'weak spot' in the dream's disguise.

When I asked her to repeat it, Sophie reported her dream almost exactly as she had the first time. But, when she described the changing room, she added another detail. 'It wasn't very big,' she said, raising her arms. 'It was like this, about the size of this room.'

'This room, my consulting room' – I raised my arms too – '*is* a type of changing room.'

She looked blank.

'It's a room where people come to change,' I said.

Sophie smiled. 'I guess it is,' she said. 'But what does that mean?'

I said that I thought her dream, her being late to my office and her sleeplessness suggested that she was anxious about our meeting.

'Aren't most people who come here?' She crossed her ankles, tucking them under her chair. 'Why would I dream about the gas chambers?'

I told her that her dream could be expressing a fear that going forward – changing – would lead to the destruction of her life with her parents.

'I don't think of myself as someone who is frightened of change,' she said.

'You want a change – to get married, start a new family. But I think you're worried that this development threatens your childhood family.'

'You don't think I want to get married?'

'I don't hear you saying that,' I said.

I told Sophie I thought she was at an impasse. She wanted to create a new family, but she didn't want to destroy her old one. While she might feel guilty for not having posted the invitations, her actions were also a way of protecting both Nick and her parents. 'If you wanted to end your relationship with him, you would have told him that you couldn't go through with it.'

'You're saying I can't go forward and I can't go back. I understand that. It's clever,' she said. But she wanted to know how to make a decision. Should she get married or not? 'I was hoping you could help me resolve this.'

Sophie wrapped her arms around herself, then looked at me. 'When will I be able to go ahead?'

'I don't know,' I said. 'You just don't seem to be able to do it now.'

'Is that it?'

I told her that I couldn't predict the future.

There was something else that struck me. 'The force of your anxiety – it feels to me to be about something much more than a wedding – as if, when you send out your invitations, you'll actually annihilate your parents.'

Sophie considered this. She told me that sometimes after saying goodbye to her parents and walking away from their house, she worried that they didn't talk to each other when she wasn't there. Whenever she brought them a problem – a money worry, a medical issue, something wrong with her flat – they seemed to grow close again. And of course, they were involved with helping her sort out the wedding.

As she spoke, I pictured a woman who over many years had come to relate to her parents through one task or another – involving them in her life's adventures – as a way of helping their marriage to survive. I told Sophie this. She was struck by my use of the word 'survive'.

Before having her, she told me, her mother had had several miscarriages. Finally, after years of trying, her mother gave birth to a baby called Anne, who was born prematurely. For her first few months of life, Anne was in an incubator at Great Ormond Street children's hospital. Six months after Sophie's parents were finally able to bring her home, Sophie's mother woke up to find Anne dead in her crib. At that point, her parents gave up any hope of having more children.

But to their great surprise – her mother was forty-one – they had had Sophie. Her parents referred to Sophie from time to time as 'our little miracle'. For as long as she could remember, Sophie was aware that her parents feared something would take her too.

I thought that this fear for her survival likely contributed to the close relationship between the three of them. It also helped us to understand her dream a little better – change threatens the family's survival.

'I can see that,' Sophie said. She sat back in her chair.

Listening to her silence, I found myself thinking that our experience of loss shapes who we are. We lose the womb and the breast to have the world and its food. We lose our mother's protection to have school, play, friends. And if we are ever to have intimacy, we will have to lose our adolescent selves, and the impossible expectations we bring to love. As time passes, we lose our younger selves, people and places, and, eventually, life itself. Ultimately, we lose everything we have loved.

Of course, this was all familiar to me from my work, and yet I'd never quite *felt*, to this degree, the necessity of letting go of the past in order to seize the present, leaving an old relationship to arrive at a new one – the unavoidable loss that is at the heart of love.

At this point in this open-ended consultation – almost ninety minutes had passed – the question Sophie brought had shifted: it was no longer should she marry Nick, but rather, would she be able to accept the losses that marriage required of her? I told her this.

Sophie let out a deep breath. 'I don't know what I'm going to do, but I do feel lighter,' she said.

Although we had only arrived at an initial understanding of her dilemma, I took this to mean that her dream had disclosed something to us, an aspect of Sophie that she hadn't seen before. This once-hidden part of herself was now available for her to think about, to try to understand.

This felt like an appropriate place to stop. I suggested to Sophie that we meet again on Tuesday evening. She agreed. It was an encouraging start.

Late Monday morning, Sophie left a message on my answering machine. She'd gone into work early, she said, collected the carrier bag, and posted the invitations. She thanked me. Our conversation had helped her come to a decision – she loved Nick and wanted to marry him. She couldn't see me on Tuesday but would ring me in the next day or two to arrange another time. 'I think it would be really helpful to come and see you again.'

I didn't hear from Sophie that week, nor the next. In fact, I didn't hear from her for many years.

2

Two years later, in 1991, a young woman describing herself as a good friend of Sophie's called me to ask for a consultation. She told me Sophie thought I would be able to help. In 1998, another woman describing herself as a friend of Sophie's asked for an appointment. It happened again in 2004. Each time, I wondered if these referrals might be a communication from Sophie, her way of telling me that she hadn't forgotten me, or that she wanted to talk to me herself but could not overcome some inner resistance. Of course, because I had not seen her in years – I did not really know her – I had no way of understanding what these referrals meant to Sophie.

3

Just before Christmas of 2015 – twenty-six years after our initial consultation – Sophie left me a voicemail. 'I'm hoping that I can come and talk to you,' she said. She sounded unsettled, so I left her a message offering her an appointment for the next day.

After dinner, I played cards with my wife and children. I kept losing, much to my daughter's delight. When the children went to bed, I continued with the book I was reading, but I found it hard to concentrate.

Saturday morning was cold and bright. After breakfast, I poured myself a fresh cup of coffee and went downstairs to prepare my consulting room – turn on the lights, adjust the radiators, put out a jug of cold water, a fresh glass – and looked at my notes from my first meeting with Sophie.

Although my office is in the same building as my home, it is a separate flat. My consulting room is distinct in other ways too. In our home, more often than not, family talk is about our immediate needs – *Can I make you a cup of tea? What's for dinner? Do you have your school bag?* But my consulting room has a feeling of time suspended in it. For forty years, the room and its contents have remained essentially the same, and this continuity seems to amplify a feeling of connection to the past. For both my patients and myself, entering my consulting room can feel like one of those ritual visits from childhood – to a grandparent's house at

Christmas, or to the same holiday cottage by the sea; the place and its objects call back moments that have flown.

Sitting in my chair, reading my notes, I tried to remember Sophie. Who was she? What was it like for her to be her? During the intervening quarter of a century, I had married, had children, and spent tens of thousands of hours in this room with patients. When I first met Sophie, I was just starting out – what did I know? It was all so long ago. Who was the thirty-seven-year-old psychoanalyst listening to her then?

At 10.15, the doorbell rang. Sophie's straight dark hair was now white, but still cut in a precise chin-length bob. As before, she wore black. We smiled and shook hands. She greeted me as if it had only been a short break, but, walking along the corridor to my consulting room, I was aware of how much older I must appear to her. She thanked me for making time for her. She hung her leather coat and heavy scarf on the back of her chair. I was tempted to note that it had been a while, but I wanted to hear how she would start.

She looked at me. 'I need to decide whether or not to end my marriage.'

4

A month ago, Nick had been the keynote speaker at a history conference in Durham. The morning after his talk, Sophie telephoned to ask how it had gone. A woman answered his mobile. 'There's nothing to worry about; he's out of intensive care and he's in his room – he's resting now,' she said.

He'd had a heart attack the previous night, at his hotel. Sophie caught the next train from Lewes. When she arrived in Durham, she went straight to University Hospital. Nick was asleep in bed with a drip attached to his arm. She spoke to the cardiologist – the woman who'd answered his mobile – who assured Sophie that Nick would make a full recovery. Sophie then took a taxi to Nick's hotel. At the desk, she told the manager that she wanted the key to Professor M.'s room; she'd come to collect his things. The manager hoped the professor was feeling better. He told Sophie that Nick's belongings were with the concierge. 'The professor's wife has already packed up their room,' he said. 'Are you a colleague?'

Sophie was shocked. She realised now that there had been clues – purchases on their credit card she hadn't recognised, a bottle of champagne that wasn't in the fridge any more. Nick had been getting more and more text messages. Once or twice, she'd caught the same unfamiliar scent in their car, or on his clothes. 'I noticed,' she told me. 'But I didn't stop to think.'

Sophie wasn't sure what to tell me about her marriage. After the wedding, they were passionate – Nick was lovely, attentive, caring. But for some reason, when the children were small, her desire for him had fallen away. She didn't know how to explain it. Where was her heart? She loved the children. She was focused on them; perhaps there just wasn't much left for Nick. Or maybe, when the children were little, they'd gone in different directions. 'Maybe we lost each other,' she said. But then, that wasn't exactly it either.

Nick worked hard at his career. She admired his commitment. 'But I don't want you to think we have a marriage where only his career matters,' she told me. 'He's made real sacrifices for our family, and for me.'

Eight years earlier, Nick had received a once-in-a-lifetime offer from an American university. It meant more money, more prestige and more time to do the work he was interested in. A lot of academics in Nick's position would have jumped at it. But it was not a good time for the family to move to California. The children were still in school and, after years of childrearing and freelancing, Sophie had landed a permanent job at an important literary festival. Although it wasn't easy for him, Nick declined the offer. For a little while, after this decision, Sophie felt closer to Nick, but then the feeling passed.

In the weeks after Nick's heart attack, Sophie couldn't bring herself to mention his affair. She noticed Nick disappearing into the bathroom with his mobile, a few furtive calls. But, for the most part, they were focused only on his convalescence. Weak from his bypass surgery, Nick was dependent on her. She cooked for him, drove him to the doctor, bathed him.

And then, over breakfast one day, Nick said that he had some papers to pick up from his office at the university. Sophie didn't believe him. He'd been texting a lot the previous evening. So she came out with it: she told him what had happened at the hotel. They were both silent for a long time.

Sophie knew the woman, she told me. They'd met at a couple of dinner parties, and she remembered Nick excitedly talking about her when she had first joined the history department. 'Apparently she's the bright young thing in the history of photography,' Sophie said. 'Millie – that's her name – not only writes, she's curated an exhibition on photography and something-or-other at the V&A. She's young, thirty-two, unmarried.'

Nick told Sophie they'd only begun sleeping together just before the conference in Durham. 'Who knows? My sense is that Millie knows what she wants, and she wants Nick,' Sophie said. 'And he says he's tempted by the idea of getting together with her, of leaving.'

But sitting with him in their kitchen, Sophie found herself unconvinced. 'I know he doesn't really want to start a whole new life with her,' she said. 'Telling our children, selling our home, buying two flats – disentangling our lives – he's not up to it. Then having children with her? I can't see it. Nick doesn't want that.'

Sophie stopped. 'I want to confess something to you. Of course, I'm hurt, jealous, a bit frightened too – but a part of me is excited. Ever since Durham, I've had the thought that this is my moment to leave. I could leave Nick now and no one would ever blame me. His affair is my "get out of jail free" card.'

The night before she contacted me, Nick had told Sophie that he was prepared to break it off with Millie. They were lying in bed together, and he'd told her he couldn't bear the idea that his family would never sit around the kitchen table again. He loved the family they'd made, their life together – the holidays, the birthdays. He told Sophie that he loved her. As he said this, Sophie panicked.

'That's why I've come to see you. I'm not sure what I should do – stay or leave?'

Sophie was quiet, waiting for my response.

I looked at the clock on my desk. We had thirty minutes left. For some time – I don't know how long – I was lost in thought. Just as I was about to ask Sophie how she explained this marriage to herself, she ended the silence – 'Mr Grosz?'

I told Sophie that I was thinking things through. I was concerned that she was putting enormous pressure on herself to make a decision. 'You've brought a number of riddles today, but you're insisting that we answer only one.'

Relaxing slightly, Sophie said that on her way to London that morning, she had been struck by the fact that she was trapped in a dilemma the exact opposite of the one she'd been in all those years ago. 'Back then,' she said, 'I couldn't decide whether to marry. Now I can't decide whether I should divorce.'

I was reminded of a passage in Proust in which he describes a water lily, and its perpetual, never-resting movement between two points. Fastened by its stalk to the riverbed, it is always being tugged back and forth. Looking at the water lily, thinking about his aunt, the narrator has the realisation that this is what traps her. Year after year, whatever the problem, she's caught up in her to-and-fro thinking, never getting beyond it. 'You're acting as though you only have two options,' I said.

'That's how it feels to me,' she said.

I recalled my first meeting with Sophie. She'd felt stuck, unable to decide between one course of action and another. We'd only broken this impasse when we saw that we were asking the wrong question. It was not whether or not she should marry Nick, but rather, would she be able to accept the losses that marriage – and love – required of her? I reminded Sophie of this change.

'So what is the right question now?'

I said I didn't know, and that it might take us some time to figure it out. I suggested we continue to meet, and that it might be helpful for her and Nick to speak to a colleague of mine, a marriage therapist.

'No,' Sophie said. 'Not yet, anyway; not until I know what I want.'

I could see the sense of that. We agreed to meet on Mondays, once a week, beginning in the New Year. We agreed on the fee. I asked her if she had any questions. She shook her head.

Then I said, 'I have one more question.'

She looked at me.

'Why didn't you come back? When we met before?'

'Come back?'

'Yes.'

Sophie stood up. 'I don't know.' She took her coat and scarf off the back of the chair. 'I was getting married, then there were the children, everything was fine, then – I don't know.'

5

From the start, Sophie seemed keen to come, grateful for our sessions. She spoke about her children, her work at the literary festival, and the deaths of her parents. She told me more about herself, her conversations with Nick, his desire to save their marriage. Week by week, I began to form a picture of her world in my mind. I also became increasingly perplexed by a consistent detail: Sophie was at least fifteen minutes late for every session, as she had been for our two consultations. No matter when she set off from home, she always misjudged the journey.

She worried her lateness would annoy me. I explained to her that I thought her lateness was unconsciously driven. 'If you were deliberately trying to be late, every once in a while you'd get it wrong and arrive on time.' I felt her unwavering lateness was a communication – unbeknownst to herself, she was trying to tell us something. Over the course of our sessions, I proposed a few explanations: she was anxious about coming; she was limiting our contact, trying to keep our work from mattering too much; by making me wait, she was trying to show me that she was in a more important relationship elsewhere. At one point, something she said led me to wonder if her lateness was an expression of despair – unable to be perfect, she spoiled what we had. We discussed all of these possibilities.

Sophie agreed with these explanations, said she found them helpful, but continued to be late to every session. After two months, I said, 'Well, at this point I guess all we can say is that for the first fifteen minutes of each session, you'd prefer to be somewhere else.'

On Monday 14 April, my notes record that Sophie arrived fifteen minutes late, then began her session by talking about a lunch with her four closest friends. She was describing them to me – where they lived, what they did – when I stopped her. I said, 'Every time you tell me about your friends, you reintroduce them; you remind me where they live, what they do. You seem to believe that I can't remember Charlotte, Emily, Helen and Jo.'

Hearing me say their names, Sophie said, was a surprise. It melted something inside her. Her mother, who could give you the provenance of every item in her antiques shop, never remembered the names of Sophie's best friends. Charlotte was 'the one with glasses', Emily the one who used to 'live over the road', Helen the one 'whose father worked at the *Economist*'.

When I saw her next, the following Monday, Sophie said that since our last session, she'd been flooded with memories from her childhood, instances of her parents' absent-mindedness. She described her feeling of embarrassment when her mother sent her to school in the wrong uniform, or when she was the last child to be picked up from the school gates. As a consequence, she grew up to be a self-reliant adolescent. Now that she was a mother herself, however, Sophie found it hard to understand how neither of her parents had known which A levels she was going to take.

Because her parents were forever memorialising Anne, the baby who had died a year before Sophie was born, Sophie found this absent-mindedness especially hurtful. Of course, she could understand why they wanted to commemorate Anne's birthday with a visit to her grave and a donation to Great Ormond Street children's hospital, but as a child, Sophie recalled feeling resentful when she was asked if she had remembered Anne in her prayers. Or, on another occasion, when she saw that her mother carried two photos of Anne in her wallet, but not one of her. Once, when she was thirteen or fourteen, she tried to talk to her mum about all this, but she was unsure what to say, or how to say it. 'It was like talking to a wall,' she said.

We discussed her parents' attachment to the dead baby, and their disconnection from Sophie. We explored the idea that while Sophie appeared to have had a normal, affectionate upbringing – in no outward way was she ever neglected – something was lacking. Was it curiosity? Her parents sent her to a good school and took excellent care of her when she was ill. There were holidays in Cornwall and regular visits to galleries and concerts. But Sophie felt uncertain if they ever really knew her or knew what she cared about.

I couldn't know their minds, and yet I began to wonder if – from the time she was born – Sophie's parents had been so frightened of her dying, so fearful of losing her, that they had skirted the details of her life, sometimes resisting seeing her, or finding it painful to hold her in their thoughts. Through no fault of their own, they couldn't bear to let her become important. Undoubtedly, this early experience would have consequences for the way Sophie loved – how could it not?

I told Sophie these thoughts, and she agreed they made sense. For the rest of the session, neither of us spoke.

The next Monday, 28 April, Sophie showed up right at the end of her appointment – we had just ten minutes left. She started to explain, then stopped. Actually, she didn't know what had caused her to be so late.

Sometimes, sitting opposite a patient, I find it easier to gather my thoughts if I let my gaze drift to the bookshelves behind them. When I looked back at Sophie, I told her that we had only a few minutes left, and that there was something I wanted to tell her.

I had been thinking about the missed minutes at the start of every session, I said. 'I think these minutes might be the most important part of our meetings.'

She asked what I meant.

I said that I'd been thinking about the riddle of all those missing years – the years between our two consultations – and of those missing moments.

I thought that she might be reluctant to give up her absences from me – and not just because she had learned from her mother that what was absent could be more important than what was there. It was also because she believed that I would think about her more if she were to become her dead baby sister, if she were to become the missing one. 'Perhaps – just as your mother preferred an absent baby to a living child – you think I would prefer an absent you to a live you.'

6

I didn't see Sophie the following week. It was a long weekend, and Nick took Sophie to a country spa hotel. When we next met, she reported that the trip had been a disaster.

One particularly upsetting row ensued when, after a nice day, and dinner together, Nick wanted to have sex and couldn't understand why Sophie rejected him. Sophie told him she felt torn. She had come to see Nick's affair as a consequence of the distance between them, a product of their marriage – but still, she wasn't going to do anything she didn't want to do. Nick felt he was being frustrated in his attempts to make a new marriage. 'Nick wants something more than just mutual forgiveness. He says that he wants us to think differently, talk more openly, have more sex, love more deeply.'

The weekend had confirmed Sophie's doubts about the marriage. More and more, she imagined their separation, pictured herself living in a flat in London, as she had in her twenties. She would be near the children and away from Nick's neediness.

'When you first came to see me a few months ago, we didn't know the right question to help you out of your impasse – whether you should stay or go. Maybe the question is: do you want to leave Nick in order to grow, or could it be a way to continue to avoid intimacy?'

'What do you mean?'

'I wonder if divorce is a way of *continuing* your marriage.'

'I really don't understand.'

I put it to Sophie that there was something alive, something passionate, about her row with Nick. Of course, like any marriage, hers was comprised of two imaginations, two narratives, and I only knew the story she was telling me – but, according to her, since January, Nick had been trying to create a new marriage with her, one in which they were closer. I reminded her that she had panicked when Nick told her that he wanted to stay in the marriage, that he loved her. 'I'm suggesting you're more wedded to your remoteness than you are to Nick.'

'You're saying that my marital problems are connected to this thing of being the dead baby, the absent one.'

'I believe you want to divorce Nick to preserve your distance – yes, your absence. Nick wants to remarry you, have a proper marriage. You're frightened of this.'

Sophie agreed that she'd always been guarded. But this distance in her marriage had made her unhappy too. She accepted what I was saying, she said, it felt right, but why would she want to remain wedded to something that caused her unhappiness?

'The gap between you and Nick does make you unhappy, but it is *familiar* – and for that reason it feels safe. Your unhappiness is safe.'

Sophie was silent for some time. After a while, I asked if she could tell me what she'd been thinking.

She tried to recollect the sequence of her thoughts. Our conversation had made her feel sad – no, depressed. Then she had been thinking about her relationships. 'I worry that because my parents never properly attached to me, I'll never properly attach. I worry there is something missing in my relationships – to the children, to Nick. And I was remembering our first meeting, those wedding invitations that I couldn't post. I was so frightened. I had that terrible nightmare.'

For a moment, neither of us spoke. On the pavement across the road a dog barked.

I thought that Sophie might be remembering our first meeting because our session that day was so very similar to that first consultation. Back then she had found she had to let go of her parents, their world of three, to make room for her new life with Nick. Now she would have to let go of a part of herself – her remoteness, this particular way of being – if she was ever to be genuinely married. I told her this.

'I see that,' she said. 'I see.'

In the weeks that followed, we continued to discuss the issues raised by this exchange. It took time – for Sophie to find the words to describe her experience, and for us to work through the implications of our new understanding. Towards the end of June, Sophie asked if I could give her and Nick a referral to a marital therapist.

In our last session before the start of my August break, Sophie came in with a sunburnt nose. She'd spent the weekend on the Sussex coast, hiking with Nick. As they walked, she'd found herself thinking about mourning. Her parents thought that mourning meant coping, she said. 'I didn't understand that mourning means accepting reality.'

7

The following Monday, the first day of my August holiday, I took my dog for an early-morning walk on Hampstead Heath. Under a wide-open sky changing from purple to orange, I thought about Sophie, our very first meeting all those years ago. I thought about my own marriage. And then I thought about the work we have to do to reach each other.

When I got home, I went to my consulting room, took out my notebook, turned to a fresh page, and began to write this story.

Lost Love

Before the internet, before email and mobile phones, a marriage therapist I knew sent me a letter requesting that I see one of his patients. The patient's name was Dr Ravi M., and he was a forty-three-year-old mathematics lecturer. Ravi and his wife were in marital therapy. The therapist thought Ravi's wife, Dr Sonal M., a physics lecturer, was anxious to improve their marriage, and committed to the treatment. He found Ravi less enthusiastic. Reticent, was how the therapist described him. He hoped individual psychoanalysis would help Ravi to be more forthcoming.

According to my colleague, there was very little collaboration between husband and wife. They didn't seem to be able to work together on small things or large ones. Ravi, for instance, refused to let his wife know when he would be home for dinner. For her part, Sonal was reluctant to go for a walk with him, see a film together or even sit on the sofa and watch a television programme. Each was stuck in their own world.

Married for ten years, the parents of two girls, aged seven

and five, Ravi and Sonal could not talk to each other about their daughters without quarrelling. At the end of his letter, my colleague added, 'They can appear old-fashioned, even prudish. The truth is they had a passionate marriage. Until recently, they were having sex at least twice a week and enjoying it. Both use words like "miraculous" to describe their sexual connection. There was passion and friendship, but something changed.' He went on: 'I believe they love each other. I think they could be happy, but something is preventing them from being a couple. Ravi's uncommunicativeness is a big part of the problem.'

At our first appointment, Ravi wanted to make sure I wasn't going to share our conversations with the marriage therapist. After I reassured him, Ravi confided, 'He thinks I'm uncommunicative, but I'm not talking for a reason.'

Just after he was born, Ravi told me, his mother became depressed, and his father moved out. His parents divorced, and his father emigrated to Canada, where he then had a second family. Ravi remained in London with his mother and grandmother. He didn't see his father again until he was seventeen years old. 'I know what divorce is. It's a catastrophe. I can't bear the idea of not living in the same house with my daughters.'

I couldn't help but say, 'If you want to avoid divorce, wouldn't it be best to talk to your wife, bring whatever problems you're having into couple therapy?'

Ravi laughed. He would never confront Sonal, he said. It was too dangerous. He loved her. He believed if they could just avoid the subject, never talk about it, they might be able to escape the cataclysm of a divorce. 'If I talk about the problem, or worse, if she starts to talk about it – that's it. We'll have to get a divorce. I don't want to hear her confess.'

'Confess what?'

Ravi hesitated, looked down at the floor between us, and said, 'Sonal is having an affair.'

He looked up. 'He's a lawyer. They live in our road. Our children are the same age; they attend the same school. His name is Rakesh.'

I waited.

He went on, 'A little over a year ago, Rakesh's wife was diagnosed with breast cancer. Sonal began taking food around to their house, helping with pick-up and drop-off. In our community, we help each other.'

Sometimes, after their daughters' dance class, when the two families were together, Ravi had seen Sonal touch Rakesh's arm when she was speaking to him. 'I didn't think anything of it. Then, about a year ago, I saw them on the pavement in front of his house. The way she was standing, her head so close to his, and the way she was looking at him – I knew they were sleeping together.'

Ravi described his inventory of unwelcome knowledge. His wife and Rakesh had sex every Friday morning in his home, in his bed. Sonal had switched her cleaning routine last April; because she'd stopped changing the sheets on Sunday afternoons and begun changing them on Friday afternoons, Ravi knew the exact date they had begun having sex regularly.

Sonal had also begun attending an exercise class at the university. She had lost weight, and started buying new clothes, new underwear. She had also begun leaving everything out for him to see – her engagement diary, receipts, bank statements. There was nothing incriminating, but this fake full disclosure only confirmed his worst suspicions. 'If she were to confess her adultery, in our home, in our bed—' Ravi stopped. 'If she told me the truth about her affair, I'd have to divorce her.'

Ravi was profoundly jealous. He was suffering in that terrible labyrinth of panic, dread and depression. I told him his feelings were a normal reaction to his wife's infidelity. I suggested we meet twice a week to think together about his feelings and desires, so that we might find a way forward.

The experience of adultery seemed to have shrunk Ravi. Although he was big – tall, broad-shouldered – there was something of a lost child about him. At our next meeting, he told me that after our consultation, when he'd left my office, he couldn't remember where he'd parked. It was some twenty minutes later, after he decided to walk home, that he remembered he hadn't driven to my office at all, he'd walked.

Ravi hated when things weren't right, by which he meant ordered, logical, defined. Ravi's grandmother, who had helped to raise him, had been a well-known mathematician in her younger days in Delhi. She'd taught Ravi that mathematics was the work of making things right. His work as a mathematician was a kind of refuge: when he solved a problem, he felt good. He felt he *was* good. Now, because he couldn't find a solution to the problem of Sonal's affair, he felt bad.

Ravi had a naïve boyishness that stirred up paternal feelings in me despite the fact that I was younger than he was, by about ten years. I felt that Ravi wanted me to be the father-protector he had lost – to stand between him and his mother's depression, or between him and his grandmother's singlemindedness, and now between him and Sonal's infidelity.

For the first two months of our work together, Ravi often talked about his loneliness, but I was particularly struck by his many anxieties: the fear that Sonal would try to speak to him about her affair; the fear that his daughters had begun to sense their mother's 'feelings' for Rakesh; the fear that he was about to lose his family. In one intense session, Ravi worried that his mother's depression and his father's leaving to start a new family were all a result of something ugly and unlovable in him.

Then one day about three months into his psychoanalysis, Ravi turned up late. He explained that someone had broken into several of the cars in his road, and the investigating police officer had asked to review the tape from the CCTV camera mounted over Ravi's front door. He and Ravi had spent the morning looking through the footage but had found nothing out of the ordinary.

I asked Ravi if he had ever looked at the CCTV tape to confirm his suspicions about Rakesh and Sonal.

'I don't need to,' he said.

'You've never actually seen Rakesh going in or out of your house? And yet you could check – that would give you clear evidence, either way.'

'I have plenty of evidence.'

'What kind of evidence?'

'I'll bring it in and show you.'

Every night after his wife fell asleep, he explained, he would retrieve her underwear from the laundry basket and inspect it for pubic hairs. One pubic hair was 'okay, acceptable'. More than one meant she'd been 'having it off'. On a recent Friday, he'd found four pubic hairs, including one that was a different colour to Sonal's – dark, like Rakesh's. He'd put this hair in an envelope, and locked the envelope in his desk at the university. 'I'll bring it next time,' he said.

'Ravi, this is crazy thinking. You can't know that your wife is unfaithful by looking at her underwear.'

'You absolutely can. On Fridays, there are more hairs. A break from the mean.'

'You keep a chart? The number of hairs? In your wife's underwear?'

'I don't need a graph, I *know*. Numbers don't lie. They tell the truth.'

Ravi's 'evidence' threw me into doubt. Was this some sort of mono-symptomatic psychosis? Was he an Othello? Maybe *he* was having an affair? I can only know what my patients tell me. Sonal did seem to have a warm relationship with Rakesh, maybe even a bit flirtatious. But Ravi had also described to me a woman who was predictable, a trustworthy mother and academic: a reliable woman devoted to her family. My spontaneous suggestion that Ravi might look at the CCTV tape to confirm whether or not Sonal was having an affair did not give him relief – he was adamant, fighting for his belief that she was unfaithful: why?

As I was having these thoughts – trying to make sense of what I'd just been told – Ravi was getting more and more worked up about his 'evidence'. When a patient is becoming increasingly agitated, I might try to direct that person away from the heat of the present, to the past.

'We only have a few minutes left, and I won't see you until next week,' I said. 'I've been thinking about you as a baby, alone with a mother who is having a breakdown, a mother falling into a severe depression. I was thinking you might have become depressed, too.'

'Can a baby get depressed?' Ravi asked.

'From everything you've told me, there were times when your mother couldn't take care of herself or you. I can imagine you depending on her, and her not responding. Yes, I think that would make a baby depressed.'

Ravi settled.

In the silence, I imagined the enormity of Ravi's distress as a baby: his father gone, his mother not responding to his cries. Ravi's delusion could be a protection against the anxiety of abandonment – a defence against trusting Sonal.

'I'm thinking,' I said, 'your convictions about Sonal's infidelity may be a way of protecting yourself against the dangers of intimacy. You're frightened of love.'

This case was confounding enough that I felt I needed a supervisor. I rang Dr Harold Stewart, a psychoanalyst I knew from my training. He had a reputation for being able to hear the thoughts and feelings a patient had not, could not, put into words. Dr Stewart had been a general practitioner for almost twenty years before retraining as a psychoanalyst, and he had a tremendous depth of experience.

Two days after my session with Ravi, I was drinking coffee in Dr Stewart's consulting room. He was broad-chested, with strong arms and dark brown eyes. The grandson of poor Jewish immigrants, Dr Stewart was born in the East End – 'within the sound of Bow Bells', he liked to say – which at the time made him the only cockney psychoanalyst in the British Psychoanalytical Society.

In a well-worn plaid shirt, soft grey trousers and old leather slippers, Harold looked as if he'd just been pottering in the garden. This was long enough ago that next to his psychoanalytic couch was a floor-stand ashtray for the use of his patients.

After settling in the chair opposite him, I told Harold about the referral, and about Ravi's personal history. Then I read out my 'he-said, I-said' account of our last session.

When I'd finished, Harold said, 'I liked you telling him his delusion was crazy thinking. You were picking up the litter. When a patient throws down a delusion, you have to pick it up, hand it back to him.'

Harold looked at his notes: 'They were having sex at least twice a week, there was passion, there was friendship. Once the delusion starts, love stops. This nonsense with the pubic hairs means Ravi's mind is flooded with pornographic images of Sonal and Rakesh – these images are overpowering his own loving thoughts of Sonal.'

Harold returned the demitasse cup to its saucer. 'A delusion is a fire that burns down reality. There will be times, like with the CCTV, when you can show him that he has been evading reality rather than seeking evidence. Just continue as you've begun: pick up the delusion, and hand it back. Help him to speak about his feelings.'

I asked Harold if he'd ever had a patient suffering from delusional jealousy.

One of his first psychoanalytic patients, he said, was a young French woman. She was married to an officer in the Royal Navy, a submariner. He lived at sea for sometimes as long as six months at a time. 'She came to believe he wasn't at sea at all, but living in Edinburgh with another woman, having a very passionate sexual relationship,' he said. 'Her delusion was destroying what had been a good marriage.'

'What did you do?'

'It was clear to me that psychoanalysis gave her a place to talk about her loneliness, her rage with her husband for leaving her, her own unfulfilled sexual desires. What worked was listening, interpreting her resistance to the analysis – and refusing to accept her delusion. I had to play a long game, but the delusion eventually disappeared. In the end, she didn't need it.'

In the months that followed, the more Ravi brought himself into his psychoanalysis – his feelings, dreams, memories of his childhood – the less he spoke about his evidence. Finally, one day, less than a year after my supervision with Harold, he stopped talking about it altogether.

Ravi and Sonal began collaborating, doing small things together – they made a habit of taking a long walk together every Sunday morning. When Ravi was offered a position at Cambridge, I was impressed that he told the University he could take up the post only if Sonal could continue her work too. These changes seemed to confirm my original hypothesis – that Ravi's delusional jealousy was protecting him from the dangers of love. When the time came for Ravi to move to Cambridge, we set a date for our work together to come to an end. While I thought he should continue his analysis – either with me or with a psychotherapist in Cambridge – I was pleased with what we had achieved.

Only many years later – after receiving an unexpected telephone call from Sonal – did I realise that my understanding of this case had been incomplete. I had missed something essential.

On 2 December 2007, two and a half years after Dr Stewart died, and nineteen years after the end of Ravi M.'s psychoanalysis, Sonal rang me to say that she wanted Ravi to come back into psychoanalysis with me.

I explained to her that I could not contact him, but that if he rang me and wanted to meet, I'd make myself available. 'Is it an emergency?' I asked.

'*I* think so.' Sonal let out a long breath. 'Long story short, two years ago I was diagnosed with ovarian cancer,' she said. She'd had surgery, done chemotherapy, and then, three months earlier, had been told the cancer had spread to her liver. 'My doctors have told me there's nothing left to try. I have months, not years,' she said.

Sonal had started chemotherapy again, but this time the aim of the treatment was simply to slow the cancer as much as possible. At times, the chemotherapy regimen was too much to bear, and she had recently found herself thinking about stopping the treatment and beginning palliative care. I started to tell her how very sorry I was, but she talked over my words of comfort.

Over the past two years, since she had been diagnosed, Ravi had become increasingly cold and withdrawn. 'Just as he was when he first came to see you,' she said. 'Now that I'm stage four, he's even worse.'

I asked her if something specific had happened.

A few weeks ago, she told me, she'd had a birthday. Her daughters had gone to a lot of effort, but Ravi had given her a card she knew had been in his desk for years, and a small bunch of flowers from the stall up the road. 'My last birthday,' Sonal said. 'But that's not what bothered me.'

Over the past two years, she said, when she'd been up at night, sick from the chemo and frightened, she'd been working on a book of family recipes. It included the dishes she prepared week-in, week-out, but also foods the girls had loved when they were small, and special dishes Ravi loved. She'd decided to include stories from the life of the family, making it a sort of family memoir. She had found photos taken during family meals – at birthdays and festivals – as well as holiday photos taken in cafés and restaurants on their travels. 'There is a wonderful photo of the four of us in New York, at a baseball game, eating pizza,' she said. 'I wanted to leave something of me – for Ravi, for my daughters, for the grandchildren I'll never know. It's my way of loving them into their future.'

Sonal hadn't told Ravi or the children about the book. A few weeks earlier, she'd had it printed and bound so that she could give each of them a copy on Diwali.

That day just after sunset – when traditionally they'd light diyas and candles – Ravi had claimed he had a headache and then said that it was probably the flu. The girls couldn't coax him back down from the bedroom. 'He spoiled the occasion,' she said.

Sonal and her daughters had curled up on the sofa – one on either side of her, just like when they were little – and read the book together. 'My daughters loved it,' she said. 'But Ravi unwrapped his copy and left it sitting on his bedside table, still in its paper. He hasn't looked inside.'

She went on, 'My therapist tells me Ravi's angry with me

because I'm dying. I get that, but I feel terribly trapped. The more I love him, the meaner he gets.'

We were both silent.

'Mr Grosz, I've tried to get him to go back into couple therapy, but he won't go. Will you please see him?'

I told Sonal that if he contacted me, I would. And then I added that if it would help, I could meet with them both.

After I hung up, I sat in my chair for a long time. Eventually I remembered my penultimate session with Ravi, nineteen years earlier.

At the conclusion of any psychoanalysis, there are certain tasks to be done. It is important, for example, that my patients know that they can return to speak to me at any time, or ask me to help them find another psychotherapist. Sometimes, I will tell my patient that if he needs further help, asking for it is a sign of success, not failure.

Often in the penultimate session – after my patient has told me his thoughts and feelings about the psychoanalysis – I will summarise my understanding of the work we have done together: what we have achieved, and what remains to be done. In Ravi's case, I reminded him that he was no longer in the grip of his delusional jealousy, and explained to him why I thought this was so. I described improvements in his marriage and work life, and his relationship to himself.

He agreed, then he was silent.

I paused for a moment, thinking how best to put my next

point. Then I said that although he'd agreed with me that there had been these improvements, he'd never once expressed gratitude. 'I have no memory of you saying thank you,' I said. 'Going forward, your inability to feel or express gratitude is something you might want to think about.'

'I express my gratitude. I pay you, don't I?' he said.

Ravi was treating Sonal as he'd treated me all those years ago. When it was time to say goodbye, he was not going to say thank you.

I emailed Sonal a month later to tell her that Ravi hadn't contacted me. She replied that Ravi's position hadn't changed. He would not return to couple therapy or come to see me. I wrote to Sonal to say how sorry I was, and to wish her well.

In the days after this email exchange, I found myself wanting to talk to Harold. I confided this to an old friend, a psychotherapist who works with the dying and the bereaved. 'Some things are best put in writing,' she said. 'If a client has something they want to say to the dead, I suggest they write them a letter.'

When I got home, I opened my computer and started typing.

Dear Harold,

I missed something important in Ravi's psychoanalysis – something dark, destructive. I didn't see Ravi's envy of Sonal's love.

Sonal wasn't a saint. By Ravi's account, she could be difficult at times, unyielding. What I didn't see was this: when she was at her most loving, he was at his most envious.

Ravi's delusion had nothing to do with ordinary jealousy. During his psychoanalysis, I'd understood his delusional jealousy as a defence, his way of protecting himself against the feelings that love entails. I can now see that Ravi's belief that Sonal was unfaithful vandalised the real love she gave him. His delusion degraded her love. It destroyed the idea of her as his loving wife. As you said: once the delusion started, love stopped.

We'll never know what triggered Ravi's delusion. Perhaps it was some specific act, or acts of love by Sonal towards him. We know it erupted after he witnessed her loving thoughtfulness towards Rakesh's wife, their children and, of course, Rakesh. The tortured and torturing ideas about Sonal and Rakesh in Ravi's mind spoiled all that and, for a time, his own marriage. This spoiling was a signal of envy. His inability to say thank you was a signal of envy. I should have seen this, and expressed it to him.

Sonal told me she feels trapped. I'm sure Ravi feels trapped too. Because his envy is unconscious, he will not know why he is doing what he is doing. He would tell you he loves Sonal, and yet, when she most needs his love, he can't give it. Or, what he is giving will not feel to her like love. Mired in his envy, Ravi can't make his way to a place where he can see himself.

I find myself coming back to these lines of poetry by Czesław Miłosz:

Love means to learn to look at yourself
The way one looks at distant things
For you are only one thing among many.
And whoever sees that way heals his heart,...

Oh Harold, I miss our conversations. I miss you. I'll miss you always.

Stephen

After finishing my letter to Harold, I realised of course that this problem belongs to all of us, not just to Ravi. At one time or another, each of us can get stuck in envy, or some kind of resentment, and in these instances, the fiction that grows up around us blocks our view: the ones we love and are closest to become characters in a world of our own imagination and we are trapped. We lose our connection to them, and they to us.

Envy, grievance, anger – these feelings can ensnare us. *How could you?... I can't believe you...Seriously?* Our eye-rolling, our tirades – spoken and unspoken – are self-valorising. Letting go of a grievance is difficult because we have to abandon our sense of superiority. It's difficult to give up the pleasures of exasperation or indignation, or what I've seen called 'the ecstasy of sanctimony'. Finding our way back to a place where we can see ourselves requires courage.

How do we do this? Miłosz's poem is a good place to start:

Love means to learn to look at yourself
The way one looks at distant things

Miłosz seems to be saying that love – like psychoanalysis – can be an instrument for self-reflection, for reconsideration: a place where we can question ourselves, our feelings, our reality.

Penetrating the familiar is hard work. One could argue that the greatest obstacle to discovering the shape of the earth wasn't ignorance, it was the 'knowledge' that the earth was flat. The greatest obstacle to learning about ourselves isn't ignorance, but our 'self-knowledge'. Love requires us to let go of how we see ourselves, to see ourselves in ways we may not like.

Ravi never returned to see me. He wanted love, yes, and he also believed he was giving love. He couldn't see himself clearly and, in the end, refused to do love's labour: the ongoing task of reconsidering our story anew. Without that work he could not see Sonal. She was lost to him, and he to her, even before the illness took her away for ever.

An Impossible Desire

1

Two years after qualifying as a psychoanalyst, I took up a post at the Portman Clinic, a forensic psychotherapy unit in Hampstead. Occasionally, I would treat the wife, husband or child of an offender, but most of the patients I saw had committed a crime themselves. Some of my patients had a history of violence. One had attacked his previous psychotherapist, but that's another story.

The Portman Clinic was run by Dr Mervin Glasser, who was my supervisor. Dr Glasser had written papers on sexuality and delinquency; aggression, incest and paedophilia. He had an enormous international reputation. He was best known for his idea of what he called a 'core complex' in all of us, composed of two contrary anxieties: engulfment and abandonment. In his view, we have from birth a deep-seated longing for an intense intimacy with others, and yet this very longing can lead to the fear of a permanent loss of self. On the other hand, our desire for independence, for self-sufficiency, can take us to a place where we fear being forgotten. These two anxieties are at work when we love. Inevitably, the beloved will fail to maintain the shifting distances we desire – they telephone too often, or don't pick up quickly enough.

When I started work at the clinic, Dr Glasser had been director of the Portman for almost twenty years – he was coming up to retirement. He was sixty-two, and I was thirty-seven. He kept a certain distance. A reserved man, he took a formal, almost solemn interest in my professional development. My first cases included the wife of a high court judge who had shoplifted bread from Harrods; a sixteen-year-old boy from Hackney who had set fire to his school; a convicted exhibitionist; a male nurse prone to sudden acts of shocking violence; and a twenty-nine-year-old barrister who had referred herself to the clinic – she travelled on the Underground in high heels, so as to be better able to cause pain when she deliberately stepped on men's feet.

One day, after a staff meeting, Dr Glasser pulled me aside to ask a favour. He wanted me to take on the case of a twenty-one-year-old woman who had just been released from prison. She'd served fifteen months for stealing nearly £30,000 from her workplace. 'I don't have a vacancy or I'd take her on myself,' he said. 'She's had the most terrible time.' There was an urgency in his voice. 'She needs help. Can I leave her file in your tray?'

Kate F.'s file was unusually thick: there were police and medical reports dating back to when she was fifteen, a social worker's statement, various witness testimonies, a psychological assessment for the Court, letters from her solicitors to the clinic among various legal documents, some correspondence between the clinic coordinator and her probation officer, as well as newspaper clippings. Here and there, stuck to these pages, were yellow Post-it notes – a number of which were marked 'urgent'.

The most recent item in the file – at the top of this stack – was a photocopy of a recent letter from a solicitor in Scotland, warning Kate not to contact a man named Alasdair F. It concluded:

> Given the history between you and Mr F., he finds your correspondence and telephone calls distressing, upsetting and unwelcome.
>
> He does not want you to write to him or to telephone him. He does not want to see you or speak with you. In short, he does not want to have any contact, of any kind, with you.
>
> As his legal representatives, we ask you to please not contact him again.

Who was this letter from? What had happened?

Deeper in the file I found Dr Glasser's Court Report. When she was seventeen, Kate got a job as an assistant bookkeeper. After a year on the job, she started pocketing some £100 a day. She didn't spend the money; she hid it in her bedroom. When she was arrested, she returned the pilfered £30,000 to her employers. Why, he asked, was Kate stealing money that she did not spend?

Kate's stealing, Dr Glasser wrote in his conclusion, was best understood as a response to emotional deprivation; it was her attempt to undo her psychological losses. She had suffered. Her crime was not committed in accordance with the claims of outer, material reality, but with the demands of inner, psychic reality. Unconsciously, she was seeking justice. Prison would not help; it would harm her. A custodial sentence, he concluded, was completely inappropriate.

The last paragraph of his report read, as it usually did when he had reasoned against a prison sentence:

> With respect, should the Court accept our advice – that Ms F. does not receive a custodial sentence – we would ask that psychotherapy *not* be made a condition of an alternate sentence. In order to be effective, therapy needs to be undertaken voluntarily. We believe that Ms F. needs psychotherapeutic help, and could benefit from it. If at any time, she asks for our assistance, we would make every effort to offer her treatment.

In the empty staffroom, I poured myself a cup of coffee, found a comfortable chair by the window, and worked my way through the file.

One of the first documents was a letter from Kate's GP. It gave a bit of family history. When Kate was eight months old, an exhausted Mr F. brought her and his wife to the GP asking for help: 'She's an easy baby; it's my wife who is always bursting into tears.'

Believing Mrs F. to be suffering from postnatal depression, the GP referred her to a specialist psychiatrist; Mrs F. refused the referral and his prescription for antidepressants. Several years later, after Mr F. discussed his deteriorating relationship with his wife, the GP suggested they speak to a marriage counsellor; Mrs F. rejected this referral, too. Against this background, the rest of Kate's life, up until the age of thirteen was – as far as her GP could tell – 'normal'.

A social worker's report, based on interviews with Kate and her mother, described what happened next. Saturdays were her mum's busiest days at the salon, so Kate spent them with her dad. Typically, around noon, Kate and her father would go to the pub for lunch – they both had fish and chips – then they would walk along the Thames to Stamford Bridge to watch Chelsea play.

One Saturday a few months before she turned fourteen, just before her mother left for work, Kate's parents had a row. From her bedroom, Kate could hear her mother crying, shouting at her father. ('You think you're so clever.' 'You always know everything.' 'I wish you would just leave.') Then she heard the front door slam. A little while later, Kate came downstairs to find her father crumpled on the floor – he was having a heart attack. She called 999. While the ambulance rushed to their house, the operator talked her through CPR. By the time the paramedics arrived, Kate's father was dead.

The following September, Kate's uncle, her father's youngest brother, came to London to study computer science at university.

It was his first time away from home. He moved in with Kate and her mother as a paying lodger, the idea being that this would help them financially, and that he might also be able to help Kate with her studies. During the next year, the three of them got on well. According to Kate's headmistress, her schoolwork improved, especially her maths.

Kate's uncle, Alasdair, had been living with the family for nearly a year when one day in June, sick with a stomach bug, Kate's mother came home early from work. She saw Kate's school bag in the front hall. Without taking off her coat, she went upstairs. On reaching the landing, she saw Alasdair coming out of Kate's room. Later, she would tell the social worker that she couldn't understand why he was barefoot. Alasdair began to talk to her, saying something; she pushed around him. Opening Kate's door, she peered in. The room was in shadows. A sticky-sweet smell from an apple-scented candle filled the room. Kate's mother stood still, letting her eyes adjust. Kate was standing next to her unmade bed, buttoning up her school blouse. At her feet, in a jumble, her mother could now make out Alasdair's socks.

'We weren't hurting anyone,' Kate said.

Her mother went downstairs and telephoned the police.

Kate told the police that a month or two after Alasdair moved in, late at night, when she was frightened and couldn't sleep, she would soundlessly make her way to his room. 'When I was little, my mum got angry with me when I tried to get into bed with her and Dad – she said my tossing and turning kept her awake.

Dad would walk me back to my room, tuck me in, and sit on the floor next to my bed until I was asleep. She didn't like me coming into her bedroom. I could get into Alasdair's bed without waking him.'

Her testimony – written up by the female detective constable who interviewed her – went on:

Q: Where did he touch you?
A: For a long time, we didn't do anything. We cuddled.
Q: Then he did touch you?
A: Yes.
Q: Where did he touch you?
A: All over.
Q: Where precisely?
A: Round here. (Indicating her breasts and vagina.)
Q: Do you remember the date, when he started touching your vagina?
A: I don't remember. It wasn't right away. We cuddled together for a long time.
Q: A long time?
A: Six months. No, longer. More than six months.
Q: Did he ever put his penis inside you?
A: Yes.
Q: When did this happen?
A: Just after my birthday, that's how I remember.
Q: Just after your fifteenth birthday?

A: *Yes.*

Q: Your uncle would have been nineteen years old at that time?

A: *I don't know – yes.*

Q: Did your uncle ever threaten you?

A: *No, never.*

Q: Was it frightening when he put his penis inside of you?

A: *No, not in a bad way.*

Q: In what way?

A: *I was frightened we'd get caught.*

The next document in the file was Alasdair's witness statement to the same female detective. He described feeling hurt and betrayed – 'How can they do this to me?' Simultaneously, he blamed Kate ('she used to get into *my* bed'), and rationalised their relationship ('she's older than Juliet, in *Romeo and Juliet*'). Written up by the detective, his testimony continued:

Q: Can you tell me about your previous sexual relations?

A: *It was the first time for both of us.*

Q: Did Kate ever object to you putting your penis inside her vagina?

A: *Mostly we cuddled.*

Q: Did Kate ever object to you putting your penis inside her vagina?

A: *We didn't do that until much later – mostly, we just cuddled.*

Q: I'm going to ask you that question again: did Kate ever object to you putting your penis inside her vagina?
A: *No, we both wanted to – I wouldn't have done it if she didn't. I wouldn't ever hurt her. I love her.*

Several months later, Alasdair was sent to prison, and put on the sex offenders register. He wanted to remain in contact with Kate, but the Court forbade him from doing so.

When Kate was seventeen, she left school. Hearing that she was good at maths, one of her mother's co-workers helped her get a job as an assistant bookkeeper, at a Soho fashion company. Soon after starting, Kate began to have sex with her supervisor, a married man in his early forties. His wife discovered the relationship, and he left the company. Kate's embezzling began shortly after he left. With the exception of £100 – which she accidentally left in a carrier bag on a bus – the £30,000 that she stole was recovered, from a trunk hidden in the back of her closet, and returned to her employers.

It was unclear to me what happened at Kate's trial. From her file notes, I suspected that she might have appeared to the judge as defiant, perhaps even insolent. Whatever the cause, the Court ignored Dr Glasser's recommendation. Found guilty, Kate was sentenced to fifteen months in HM Prison Holloway, the largest women's penitentiary in Europe.

Behind me, the kettle whistled. The evening receptionist had arrived. I'd been reading for a couple of hours.

I wrote a letter to Kate, offering her an appointment.

2

At our first meeting, I began by telling Kate that I knew something about her from the various reports I'd read, but it would help me if she could tell me about herself.

She said that she was having a hard time. She couldn't find a job. Last Saturday evening, she'd gone for a drink with a neighbour, a friend of the family – 'I like older guys' – and this had led to a row with her mum. She wanted to move out. She was staying with her mother, but she hated it – she didn't like her mother, she wasn't like her – and she hated her mum's boyfriend. He was always hanging around in the kitchen or sitting room, drinking beer, smoking. Kate hated cigarette smoke. 'My mum and I don't get on,' she said.

'She's tough,' Kate said. 'Her whole family's that way – cold.' During the fifteen months that Kate was in prison, her mum only visited her four times. 'What kind of a mother does that?'

'Were you ever close?' I said.

'She wasn't easy to be close to,' Kate said. 'If I accidentally spilt something, or if I tripped, fell – she'd shout at me. My dad used to say she couldn't help it.'

'You felt closer to your dad,' I said.

She was silent for so long – sitting back in her chair, looking down at the floor – that it seemed to me she might not answer.

When she raised her head, I could see that her eyes had filled with tears. After a moment or two, I asked her, 'Can you tell me what it was that made you cry?'

Kate shook her head. 'I don't like talking about my dad.'

'To anyone?' I asked.

Again, Kate shook her head no.

'Your mum?'

'No, especially not her. She was always having a go at him. We hadn't even had the funeral, and she gave all his clothes away, everything – she took it all to the charity shop. She didn't tell me, I didn't get to keep anything.'

'That sounds awful for you,' I said.

Kate did not reply. We sat in the quiet. At some point, I heard the door across the hall open, then my colleague's footsteps in the corridor. A minute or two later, I heard her making her way back to her office, then the sound of her consulting-room door clicking shut.

'Do you have a radio?' Kate said.

'A *radio*?'

'It's just so quiet in here,' she said.

I was surprised, but not *that* surprised. A number of the patients I'd seen at the Portman Clinic had little or no experience of being in a quiet room, the telephone off, alone with someone who was waiting to hear whatever they had to say. Kate's question made me think that my comments, listening, or perhaps it was the clinic's hushed atmosphere of quiet attentiveness – something about the consultation or the place – was just too much for her, and it would be easier for her if we would just listen to something else. I said this to her.

She smiled. She told me that she wasn't used to talking about her dad, and anyway, she didn't see how this was going to help her. How was just talking going to help?

We would be talking and thinking together, I said, trying to make sense of some of the things that had happened to her.

'Like why I stole the money?'

'Do you have some ideas about that?' I said.

'You know I didn't spend any of it.'

'How do you explain that to yourself?' I asked.

She didn't know what to make of it, she said. She kept the money in an old trunk in her closet. When she was little, the trunk had been her dressing-up box. 'You probably won't believe me, but after I put the money in the trunk, I didn't think about it.'

She wasn't sure how it started, or why she did it – she wasn't dishonest. There was just a lot of cash coming in each day, and she thought they wouldn't miss it. They didn't. Most days, she took about a hundred quid. Twice each day, in the morning and afternoon, her boss went down the road to get coffee. She'd wait till he was out then 'accidentally' knock a pile of notes onto the floor. Bending down, positioning herself so that her desk was between her and the office door, so that should her boss unexpectedly return she could not be seen, she'd gather up the notes. As she did so, she'd count five twenties, then push them deep into her boot, or slip the notes over the top of her jeans, into her knickers. 'I was so frightened about getting caught – my heart was pounding so hard.'

The clandestineness, the corporeality of Kate's stealing, made me think of her silently making her way to Alasdair's room. Kate had not mentioned Alasdair to me, I'd only read about him in her file – I would wait for her to bring him up. I simply told her that I thought the feelings she got when stealing – the secrecy, the excitement – might be her way of not feeling depressed.

Kate nodded too quickly, I thought, as if she was agreeing in order to sidestep thinking with me about the idea. I tried again. 'Having the money wasn't that important to you. The excitement, the heart-pounding fear seems to have been the important part – an end in itself, not a means to an end. I was thinking that the stealing itself was a kind of antidepressant.'

'Yes', she said. 'I understand that.'

I glanced at my watch; the hour was almost over. I felt that we'd made a start. I asked her if she was free to meet at this same time the following week, and she was. I explained that if she wished, this would be our regular time to meet. We would meet for fifty minutes each week. She agreed. Then I asked her if she had any questions. She said that she couldn't think of anything. We stood up, said goodbye, and she left.

The following week, I collected Kate from the waiting room. After a few minutes of silence, I asked her, 'Can you tell me what you're thinking?'

For a long time, she didn't reply. I began to think she either hadn't heard my question or was choosing to ignore it.

'I was thinking that it is nice to be here,' she said.

I asked her if there was anything from our meeting last week that had stayed with her.

She shook her head. 'No, not really,' she replied. Kate adjusted herself in the chair opposite me. Tucking her legs underneath her, she tilted her head so that her hair fell forward, hiding most of her face from view.

We sat in silence for a while. Then I told her that in my experience, the best way for us to get to know her would be if she could say whatever came into her mind – no matter how painful, absurd or embarrassing. 'Dreams, daydreams, feelings you don't understand, thoughts that make you uncomfortable – I know it is difficult, but if you can do this, it will help us both to get to know you.'

Kate looked up at me. 'I don't have any dreams,' she said and fell silent.

Although it was midday, it was overcast and gloomy. Light in the consulting room came from two standing lamps and an old black Anglepoise lamp that sat on the grey institutional desk behind my chair. Both sash windows were open a few inches at the bottom, and from a nearby school, I could hear children shouting, tumbling out onto the playground – the start of lunchtime. Catching myself, I returned to the consulting room. I was inclined to ask Kate a question, there was much that I wanted to know – about her relationship to her father and mother, friends, her daily life now – but I held back. I didn't want to be too probing, or directive.

There had been a change from our first meeting. While I didn't feel that Kate was deliberately withholding, she seemed to me preoccupied. I reassured myself with the thought that we were at the start, with time she would come to trust me, talk in a more open way about her life.

With some five minutes left, I asked Kate if she could tell me about what she was thinking. For a while she didn't reply, stroking instead, with the tips of her fingers, the fringe of her scarf. Eventually, she looked at me, and shook her head no.

Silence in a psychoanalytic session is not unusual, and yet, as the hour drained away, I felt a growing sense of uselessness. I had the thought that Kate was giving me an experience of what it was like to be her, so I said: 'I was thinking that by being quiet today, not speaking, you were communicating to me something of what it is like to be you – that you feel you live in a world that is silent, unavailable to you.'

She smiled, her eyes looked at me, unblinking, but she didn't reply.

A minute or so later, just before the hour was up, Kate said, 'Do you know about Alasdair and me?'

'I know a little bit, what's in your file,' I said.

'I'm going to write to him. His solicitors have told me not to, but I miss him, and I'm sure he still loves me.'

'This is important, but there's just a minute left,' I said.

'Do you think it's okay to write to him?'

'This is urgent for you, but there isn't time to discuss this properly today.'

'So you're telling me not to write to him?' she said.

'I'm just trying to understand why you might have left this till the very end of your session. Maybe part of you wanted to talk to me about Alasdair, or writing to him, and another part of you didn't.'

'I didn't bring it up at the end on purpose. I just remembered.'

'I agree. I think it was done unconsciously, not deliberately,' I said. 'Maybe you brought it up at the very end of the session because you want to write to him, and you're worried I'll try to stop you.'

'You won't?' she asked.

'I'm not here to prevent you from doing anything. I'm here to think about things with you.'

I looked at my watch. 'I know it feels like a long time to wait – but if you can, we can talk about Alasdair and writing to him next week.'

'We have to stop?' she said.

'Yes, it's time.'

'Right now?' she asked.

Nodding, I stood up.

'That's it?'

I nodded again. 'Yes, until next week.'

Kate remained curled up in her chair. She looked absorbed in thought. I presumed she was thinking about her letter, possibly accepting the idea of waiting a week to send it.

Then she stood up and took two quick steps forward – too close. She reached forward to flick some fluff off my jacket.

'Is it your lunch break now?' she asked.

I stepped back.

'I was just thinking,' she said, tilting her head to one side, 'that if there was a pub nearby, we could have lunch together.'

I said: 'You want us to keep talking, but we can't – we have to wait until next week.'

'I know,' she said, 'but you've been so nice to me. I just want to be nice to you.'

A realisation began to form. Her difficult relation to her mother, the death of her father, her incestuous relationship to her uncle, the affair with her boss, the stealing, this sudden come-on – these incidents were linked. I wasn't sure how to talk to her about what I was beginning to understand, but I knew what I was supposed to say. 'It's time,' I said. 'We have to stop.'

Kate shifted. 'I'd like. . .' she said, and hesitated. She continued to move, rocking, from her left foot to her right. I sensed her gathering herself up, readying herself to cross some threshold. 'Can I hug you?' she said.

I raised my right hand to signal stop.

'It's time,' I said.

Her lips turned down like a child's and she fixed me with her eyes.

Speaking softly, I said, 'I'll see you next Tuesday, we can continue then.'

She came right up, under my chin.

'Never mind,' she shouted. I felt her breath. 'Never. Fucking. Mind.'

As she grabbed her things and moved for the door, she went on shouting at me, 'You're so stupid, so stupid. You're so *fucking* stupid.' She slammed the door behind her.

I just stood there, going over what had happened. I have no idea how much time passed.

I went to the staffroom, made myself a mug of tea, came back to my office, and wrote up the session.

Then, I wrote a short note to Dr Glasser, describing what had happened, and put it in his tray. He replied straightaway, suggesting that we discuss it at our next regular supervision meeting – hopefully, he said, Kate would come to her next session.

She didn't show up, nor did she call the clinic to cancel. Following my usual practice, I wrote to her:

> I'm sorry not to have seen you today. I think I understand some of your reasons for not attending, but I would like to know more. Please come next Tuesday at your regular time.

3

When I knocked on the door to Dr Glasser's office, I felt uneasy, apprehensive, anticipating his disappointment. His office was the largest consulting room in the clinic; high ceilings and tall Victorian windows made it airy, bright, inviting.

Dr Glasser sat at the head of the table. He stood to greet me, motioned me into the chair nearest him. 'Have you heard from your patient?' he asked.

I shook my head. 'Not a thing.'

Dr Glasser found a fresh pad of paper. Taking the cap off a biro, he said, 'Let's just go straight to the sessions.'

As I read out my account of my two meetings with Ms F., Dr Glasser took notes. Several times, he asked me to repeat one of our exchanges.

When I finished, Dr Glasser was quiet. He flipped back to the first page of his notes and began reading slowly. 'That's fine,' he said. 'Yes, this is fine. I don't see much that I would have done differently.'

'Really?' I said. 'I thought things went well in the first meeting. I really didn't see it coming, the way the second session ended...'

Dr Glasser smiled. 'Your patient may have acted out in the second session precisely because there was good emotional contact between the two of you in the first meeting – it could be a negative therapeutic reaction.'

'Wouldn't she have done better with Sharon or Anne?' I asked.

'I don't think so,' he said. 'An awful relationship with her mother, no women friends, she refused an appointment with the prison's female counsellor – she detests her probation officer. It might have played out differently with a female analyst, but not necessarily better.'

'It couldn't have played out worse,' I said.

'If you mean the end of the second session,' he said, 'I think that was well handled. After she touched you, if you'd said to her, "Please sit down, let's take a few minutes to talk about this" – that would have been wrong. That would have ruined her therapy. You'd have been signing up to a shady side-deal: you flirt with me, I'll give you more time. She needs you to have boundaries, so she can too.'

Dr Glasser leaned forward. 'By ending the session the way you did, you were saying to her: "I think you can wait, I believe you don't have to act impulsively – you can use your mind to understand your feelings and control your desires." That's therapeutic.'

'Mervin, thanks – but is it therapeutic if I lose the patient?'

'You don't know that she won't return,' he said. 'Patients come into therapy in all sorts of ways. Especially young people – they start, they stop. If she *never* returns, that would be a failure, but I'm confident she'll be back.'

'I feel I should have been able to find the right form of words – something – that would have allowed her to return the following week.'

He looked at me. 'Stephen, you're thinking too much about what you said to her. It's not what you say that matters – it's what the patient hears. You have to hear what she is hearing.'

He filled a tumbler with water. 'Our patients are here because their ways of coping have failed,' he said. 'Making you feel a failure is one way your patient has to communicate to you what it is like to be her. But I suspect she may have been enacting, performing something she could not put into words.'

'Is that how you understand the end of the session?' I asked him.

'Her reaching out to touch you?'

'Yes.'

Dr Glasser put his pen down on the table. 'Some people struggle with words,' he said, 'especially people who have suffered trauma. What I mean is that some patients will find it difficult to put their feelings into words. Trauma makes you a difficult person to get along with – you suddenly get angry, shut down. People who have been traumatised speak with their bodies, with silence.'

He went on, 'For the most part, when you or I get angry, we'll use our words. We might swear or shout – eventually, we might pound the table.' At this point, he made a fist and, in an exaggerated way, pretended to bang the top of the table.

'The table represents the person we wish to hit,' he said, continuing to gently thump the surface. 'Your violent patient' – a male nurse I was treating who regularly got into fights – 'he gets angry, then, almost instantaneously, he punches the person who triggered his anger. He cannot symbolise his anger or the body of the other. He has a kind of psychosomatic reaction. He has a feeling for which he has no words – his body reacts.'

'Do you think this is what happens when her eyes fill with tears?' I asked.

'I'm thinking about her jumping up to touch you, her reaction at the very end of the session. I think she did what she did because she didn't have the words.'

'To describe feeling rejected?'

'Of course, she felt rejected,' he said. 'But – I think she is trying to represent a desire which is impossible for her to represent.'

I nodded. 'She wants to revive her father,' I said.

'My intuition is that you're right, that's true, but I'm thinking about something else: why does she want her father?'

He flipped through his notes. 'At the end of the session, she presents you with a problem. She was going to write to Alasdair. You tell her that the two of you can talk about Alasdair and writing to him next week. Perfect. That's all fine. Then she says, "Do we have to stop right now?"

'Developmentally,' Dr Glasser said, 'your patient is an infant. Although she presents as a young woman, psychologically, emotionally – her disposition towards you is infant-like.' He was speaking softly, but his deep voice, his words, had urgency. 'She wants the relationship to you that a baby has with her mother.'

He went on. 'During the session you've been there for her – listening, reflecting, trying to understand her. At the end of the session, when you say it is time to stop, you do something essential. You demonstrate to her that while you are a mother in a one-to-one relationship to her, you're also a mother in a relationship to reality, the reality of time, the rules of therapy – her fifty-minute session is finished. Her reaction is immediate, physical. She jumps up to touch you, flirts, invites you to lunch. She wants you to let go of your rules, turn away from reality. She wants to stay with you. She wants to have you all to herself.

'Then, it happens again. You say – let me find it – here, you start to have your ideas about the death of her father, her sexual relationship to her uncle, the affair with her boss, the stealing – these components come together in your mind.'

Looking up, over the top of his metal-framed glasses, Dr Glasser said, 'You confer with your psychoanalytic self. Your patient senses this internal dialogue – absorbing you, taking you away from her. Again her reaction is instantaneous, physical, she begins to rock from side to side, from one foot to the other; she asks if she can hug you. When you raise your hand to say no, she is furious. She's a rejected infant. All this is important because it gives us a glimpse of her internal world.'

Dr Glasser carefully poured water into his glass, then passed me a tumbler. 'From my interview with her, the various reports, these sessions with you – I suspect that when she was a baby, she suffered many small rejections. Often what damages a child is not a single trauma, but the accumulation of numerous injurious moments – cumulative trauma. Hidden in plain sight, mostly imperceptible to others, recurrent, tiny cuts. We know that Ms F.'s mother experienced her daughter as a burden, repeatedly pushing her away, turning from her, rejecting her. Her mother wasn't deliberately cruel; she was struggling herself, probably depressed.'

He went on, 'At a very young age, I think your patient learned to turn to her father for mothering – she took herself, her anxieties, to him. His death must have been a terrible blow to her. Since then, she seems to be trying to find a compassionate mother in men. Alasdair, her boss – these men mistook this longing for sexual desire; *she* may have mistaken it for sexual desire. Her attempts to cope with the loss of her father have made things worse for her, causing her additional trauma – she should never have been incarcerated. Her behaviour at the end of her session communicates something that she cannot represent in words: your patient wants you to be the mother she never had – a mother no one has ever had – a mother who exists entirely for her. An impossible desire.'

He rested his fingers on the rim of his glass and turned it as he spoke.

'Of course, I could be wrong. This is just a hypothesis. But it's based on what I think you were feeling your way towards at the end of her session. At a minimum, we know she wanted to stay with you – but I think we glimpsed something more. Anyway, this is the sort of thing I would be thinking about if I were in your place. When she returns, you'll listen to her – the two of you will find your own way of understanding what happened. Sometimes a start like this can be a good beginning—'

I stopped him. 'Why are you so sure she will come back?'

'I'm not sure,' he said. 'But she's suffering. She knows you want to help.'

'Won't she feel too embarrassed? She left feeling hurt. It felt final to me.'

'Perhaps, but you weren't trying to shame her. I think she heard that.'

'I'm sorry, Mervin, I just don't see her coming back, I really don't.'

'If she doesn't attend next week, write to her again. Then, the following week, after her third missed session, write to her – tell her you are sorry she is finding it difficult to come and speak with you at this time, but when she is ready to return, there is a place for her here. Tell her that there will always be a place for her here.'

Dr Glasser was looking at something over my shoulder, and I turned to see it was a small plastic alarm clock on his desk. It was time. He pushed his chair back, and stood up, signalling to me that the supervision was at an end.

I stood up and gathered my things.

'That wasn't a failure. It was good work,' Dr Glasser said, in his soft, open voice. 'You haven't seen the last of her.'

That night, I had a vivid dream. Kate was in it. We were walking towards each other from opposite ends of Waterloo Bridge. We were happy to see each other. Kate greeted me warmly. When she spoke, it was in some foreign language, which I found I had no trouble understanding.

When I woke, I lay in bed and thought about the dream. Walking in opposite directions, the location – a bridge named after a great battle – our pleasure seeing each other again. These elements needed no further analysis. The fact that she spoke in a foreign language I was able to understand put me in mind of Dr Glasser's corrective: 'You have to hear what she is hearing.'

From birth, we are raised to conceal our complex, inner lives; no matter what we feel about our mother and father, we're told we love them. Between what we feel and what we are told we should feel there is a gap. Our desires are created in this split.

To be human is to be uncertain, conflicted, divided, and yet, we grow up in a world that tells us we should feel whole, certain of our sexual desires. Brought up on the callow, familiar storylines of popular culture, encouraged to see love through the starry-eyed clichés of social media and celebrity news – we're diverted from asking ourselves the awkward questions: what is my desire? Why is my sexual self as it is? Easy stories obscure the hard ones. 'I like older guys' might conceal 'I want a man who will be the mother I never had'.

Psychoanalysis too has its own predictable narratives, but when done properly, it does not provide ready answers. Instead, it offers a place where two people can be ruthlessly honest, think together, find meaning together. If I could hear what Kate was hearing – understand her unconscious language – I might have a chance of helping her see other people as they are, not as she feared, or wished.

Six months after Kate stormed out, I received a routine reminder from the clinic secretary asking staff members to return the files of those patients not currently in treatment. At the bottom of my tray, I found Kate's file. As I was writing a closing note, I recalled my supervision with Dr Glasser, and my dream. Something was missing.

I realised that my dream interpretation was half-finished. My reading left unanalysed *why* I had the dream – why *that* dream, at *that* particular moment? Yes, I was keen to help Kate – I wanted to remedy a horrifying injustice – she should never have been sent to prison. But with a little more distance, I saw the dream as expressing a pretty obvious desire to please Dr Glasser. Suddenly, I recognised the fact that more than clinical supervision, I wanted Dr Glasser's approval. I'd brought him, not just my work with Kate, but also my frustrating relation to my own father. Unconsciously – even now it is embarrassing to admit – I wanted Dr Glasser to make me whole by giving me what a father gives a son. I was asking him to be someone he could not be, fix something he could not fix: an impossible desire.

4

Three years later – in Hampstead, on the Tube platform – I heard a voice ask, 'Mr Grosz?' I turned around. It was Kate.

She was carrying an infant, facing-out, in a baby carrier. She looked different, but I wasn't sure how. After we both expressed surprise, she put her hand on the front of the baby carrier. 'This is Freddie; Freddie, this is Mr Grosz,' she said, and added, 'You know I'm back at the Portman?'

'I didn't know that,' I said.

'Dr Glasser told me that you'd left the Clinic,' she said. 'So I'm seeing him, once a week.' She smiled.

'He's a wonderful therapist,' I said.

Kate looked down.

From the dark tunnel, the familiar, warm gust of grit, the increasing roar, the two white headlights – Kate's train stopped. The doors slid open.

'This is us,' she said. They stepped inside. As the doors closed, she waved and said goodbye.

Carnal Knowledge: Three Cases

1

Before sitting down in my consulting room, Matt A. stepped forward and shook my hand. He was an athletic and handsome forty-seven-year-old man. He wore a white cashmere jumper, black Chelsea boots and tortoiseshell glasses. His red watchband matched his socks.

Typically people who come to see me for a consultation begin by describing a problem; Matt began by describing himself. He told me that he worked in Downing Street as a political strategist and consultant for Tony Blair. This was 1999. He had been married for twenty years and had three teenage children. He described his family – his wife, Jemima, a barrister, and his two sons and daughter – with tenderness and detail. He had a season ticket to Tottenham Hotspur football club and loved to take his children to watch Spurs at the weekend, and then come home and cook for them. He especially enjoyed it when the children joined him in the kitchen, put on some music, and bopped around.

He gave me vivid, affectionate portraits of his parents – his mother was a professor of German language and literature, and his father was a linguist now working as a civil servant at Government Communications Headquarters (GCHQ). Matt was part of a close, extended family, sixteen in all: his parents, their three children, their spouses, and eight grandchildren. This group celebrated Christmases together, and spent two weeks every summer in St Ives at his parents' summer house. Matt was proud of his children's close, loving relationship with their cousins and family.

Matt was successful and happy at work. The picture of his life was buoyant.

'Tell me why you're here,' I said.

He sat in silence for a while. 'I had sex for the first time when I was sixteen. It was with a girl, a friend of my sister. A few days later, I had sex with a friend from school, a boy.'

Until his final year at university, he had regularly slept with both women and men. In his last term, he met Jemima. She was also on the History and Modern Languages course. When things got serious between them, she broke off a two-year relationship with a postgraduate student to be with Matt. Matt stopped having sex with other women but continued to have sex with men. During their twenty-year marriage, except in the months after the children were born, he and Jemima had sex once or twice a week. He also had sex, once or twice a week, with men.

He loved Jemima, he explained. He enjoyed her enjoyment of sex, her having an orgasm, but for him, only sex with men was sex. It was 'disinhibited', he said.

I asked Matt if Jemima knew he felt this way.

He'd been open with her from the start, he explained. The first time they slept together, he'd told her that he also had sex with men. 'Oscar Wilde, Alan Turing, Joe Orton – the biographies on my bedside table were a bit of a giveaway.' He'd always been honest – he had to be; they were both worried about HIV and other sexually transmitted diseases. 'She doesn't want to know the details, and I don't volunteer them. I tell her, "I have a meeting after work." She understands.'

I waited for him to say more. He explained that he felt marriage and sex were antithetical to each other. 'Gay marriage is a contradiction in terms,' he said. 'If it's a marriage, it's not gay.'

'Does Jemima know how you feel about marriage and sex?' I asked again.

'I'm not going to hurt her deliberately,' he said. 'I love her.'

'But you haven't told her the truth.'

'I haven't lied to her.'

Because he hadn't told Jemima an outright lie, Matt believed he was being honest. Jemima appeared to accept his desire for sex with men – her rule seemed to be no sex with other women. Because he didn't want to hurt her, Matt hadn't told her he preferred sex with men. I remembered something Freud wrote: 'Where they love they do not desire and where they desire, they cannot love.' I thought this might be Matt's predicament, and told him so.

He disagreed. He told me that he loved Jemima, and that he loved many of the men he had sex with too. Love, Matt told me, is an equivalence of power, an agreed understanding between two people about their desires. This equality can last years – as it had between him and Jemima – or a few minutes during a brief intense sexual encounter. 'Love ends when the balance of power breaks down, when one partner feels exploited.'

'I think you're describing intimacy,' I said.

'Aren't they the same thing?'

'The important thing is *you* think they're the same thing.'

We came to the end of our time together. I didn't know what Matt wanted from me or psychoanalysis. So, I asked him.

'I can see how other people feel – I don't feel that way.'

'Can you say more?' I asked.

'I feel slightly unreal,' he said. Then he fell silent.

Matt had created a way of being which kept certain aspects of himself cut off from each other. In his most intimate relationships, he was never altogether himself. 'Are you asking for my help to be gay?' I said.

'I would never leave Jemima and the children. Separation is not on the menu.'

'Are you asking for my help to give up sex outside your marriage?'

'Why should I?'

I tried again. 'You want me to help you accept your bisexuality.'

Matt looked at me as if I'd lost my mind.

'So I can wear a pink T-shirt and attend Pride? Are you joking? Why would I want to be bi?'

'Maybe what you want,' I replied, 'is a place where you can bring all of yourself.'

Matt sat back in his chair, his posture softened. He agreed.

To make sense of how and why we have sex the way we do, we must look closely at our personal history, especially our earliest relationships. Deeply buried or hidden in plain view, our feelings about these attachments guide our sexual behaviour much later in life. In a way, our sex lives can be thought of as a solution to the problems given to us by our earliest fears, longings and animosities.

Over the first months of Matt's psychoanalysis, we discovered that his sexual behaviour was organised by his emotions, rather than by his sexuality (whatever that is). Matt did not think of himself as straight, gay or bisexual. As far as I could tell, he did not think about his sexuality at all. On the one hand, he treasured the deeply reassuring rhythms and rituals of his life with his wife and children. On the other hand, sex with men was an essential, intensely pleasurable part of his self. 'It's not just the sex,' Matt told me. 'If I were straight, I wouldn't have these friendships.' Over the years, he'd developed relationships with a science fiction writer from Seoul and a homicide detective from Trondheim. One of his oldest friends was a male porn star with Asperger's from the Balearic Islands.

Why was Matt's personal life organised like this? Two things struck me. Matt's sex life was busy, hectic even. The other thing:

he didn't lose his temper or get angry. When I pointed this out to him, he replied that he came from 'a long line of people who don't do anger'. His parents were 'never angry' with him.

In Matt's childhood home, experiencing feelings of hatred meant one had lost control over one's body. It was akin to temporary insanity. If Matt became angry, his parents reacted with alarm and anxiety. 'My mum reacted as if I was terrible, defective, or as if she'd failed as a mother. The atmosphere was awful.' Instead of learning how to hate, Matt learned to try not to hate at all.

Psychoanalytic research teaches us that it is vital that our children learn to express their hate and love. Parent and child must be able to hate each other appropriately. As the paediatrician and psychoanalyst Donald Winnicott points out: 'Shall I say that, for a child to be brought up so that he can discover the deepest part of his nature, someone has to be defied, and even at times hated, and who but the child's own parents can be in a position to be hated without there being a danger of a complete break in the relationship?'

In another essay, Winnicott writes: 'Without one person to love and to hate he cannot come to know that it is the same person that he loves and hates, and so cannot find his sense of guilt, and his desire to repair and restore. Without a limited human and physical environment that he can know, he cannot find out the extent to which his aggressive ideas actually fail to destroy, and so cannot sort out the difference between fantasy and fact.' If a child is not hated when he does something deplorable, then his love – when he does something lovable – will not be real to him. 'It seems he can believe in being loved only after reaching being hated.'

One day, after more than two years of psychoanalysis, Matt sent me an email. It was the first time he'd written. After complaining about something I'd said to him in that day's session, he concluded:

> You don't like me. I don't like you. Your psychoanalytic silences make me feel boorish. Whenever I try to speak to you directly, you don't respond, or your response is totally insipid. You make me feel stupid, superficial, odious and unlovable. I get it. I'm not your type of patient. You don't want to see me. You want to see someone clever and attractive. Jemima is more your type. You don't understand me. You hate me. I hate you. I'm an idiot for continuing to see you, but I do. So, I'm the fool.

At the start of his next session, Matt apologised for his email. He'd accidentally hit send. Sometimes, he explained, he'll write an email or a letter, then delete it.

I told him I was pleased he'd sent it. 'You told me what you feel,' I said. 'It must be exhausting being nice all the time.'

Matt laughed. 'It is.'

2

Abigail B.'s birth was an accident. Shortly after she was born, her father told her mother: 'You wanted her, you deal with her.' Abigail had three sisters – ten, eight and six years older – who told her this story. She didn't need to hear it. She'd always felt her father was angry with her. He was affectionate with her sisters but never with her.

Abigail was clever. She went to the local Newcastle grammar school and then to Cambridge to study classics. When she was twenty-two, she won a Fulbright Scholarship to do a PhD at the University of Chicago. After six years of postgraduate study and postdoctoral teaching, Abigail returned to England to take up a position as a university lecturer. It was a beginning, first-rung academic post.

Shortly after she started her new job, Abigail had a breakdown. When her psychiatrist referred her to me, she was on a medical leave of absence for depression. Abigail wanted to quit work altogether. In fact, after a half-dozen sessions, she wondered aloud if there might be a way to live without a regular job. When I asked her how she would support herself, she laughed. It was then that she told me that while she was a PhD student in Chicago, she was also a sex worker. (The first London psychotherapist she consulted did not believe her. 'You *feel* you were a prostitute,' Abigail reported her saying.)

When she was fifteen, Abigail told me, she fell in love with boys. She loved the way they knocked about together, their restlessness and daredevilry. 'I craved excitement and I found it hanging around boys,' she said. At university, she'd had a succession of boyfriends. When she left Cambridge to start her PhD in Chicago, she found herself feeling isolated, lonely. She was also anxious about money, and didn't want to ask her father for help. During her first term, Abigail became friends with another graduate student who made extra money dancing downtown at a place called The Candy Store. The Candy Store was a front for a brothel. After several months of nude-dancing behind glass in a booth, Abigail started working in the brothel.

'Men would come to reception,' Abigail said. 'They were mostly from the financial district, college grads. We'd come out, line up, then the client would make his choice.' She continued: 'I wasn't the prettiest or the sexiest, but I was the girl most men chose.' She went on: 'Men chose me because I looked like what I was: a university student. Young. Bookish. I'm blonde, wholesome. I had a bit of puppy fat. I didn't wear much make-up. I don't have tattoos. I didn't wear lingerie or heels; I wore a white T-shirt and white pants. I looked like someone they'd want to date.'

Soon, Abigail had regulars. 'I gave one hundred per cent,' she said. Clients fell in love with her. Money poured in. 'Watching it literally pile up was *so* gratifying; for the first time in my life, way more was coming in than going out.' But there was more than money to the job. Abigail tutored the son of one workmate; when another co-worker's four-year-old son unexpectedly died of a congenital heart condition, she cared for her and helped arrange the child's funeral. Abigail felt valued.

After Abigail finished her PhD, her thesis adviser encouraged her to apply for a new lectureship in London. As best I could tell, Abigail hadn't thought about how she would feel without the community she'd created in Chicago. She threw herself into her new job, but, after several months, she struggled to sleep and eat. A panic attack sent her to her doctor, who put her on antidepressants and referred her to a psychiatrist. Worried about Abigail's anorexia and her thoughts of suicide, he changed her medication and asked me to see her five times a week. Soon, her mood stabilised.

After several months of psychoanalysis, Abigail began a session by telling me the Greek etymology of the word 'antidote': a remedy counteracting poison. Then she said: 'Sex work was an antidote to my father.' Each time a client chose her, Abigail felt 'special'. When Abigail gave a client an orgasm, she felt she had 'looked after him', 'quieted him', 'made him happy'; if he became a regular, she'd 'won him over'. These were the very feelings she'd longed to have with her father. 'Sex work cured me of my father.'

Sex work, I told her, had not cured her of her father. He still filled her mind. We discussed him more than anyone else. Because her father did not love her, she hated him. Another way to understand her sex work was as a consuming revenge drama directed at her father. Abigail then remembered that sometimes, when seeing clients, she would catch herself thinking: 'I get to do this, and you can't stop me.' At the time, she thought the sentence was some bit of 'mental chatter'. Now, she realised, she was probably speaking to her father. After a silence, she said: 'I'm talking to him in my head all the time.'

She let out a long breath. 'I don't see how we will ever change this,' she said.

'We'll do what we just did,' I said.

'What does that mean?'

'We recognise the problem. Take it seriously.'

'Then?' she said.

'Then we talk about it.'

3

Mary C. was four years old when her pregnant mother suddenly died. Two years later, her father died of a heart attack. Mary was sent from Dublin to live in a village in County Sligo with her mother's devout Catholic parents. She attended the local Catholic primary school, and regularly attended Mass.

As long as she could remember, Mary had wanted to live in a community of women. When she was nineteen, a cousin – recently ordained as a priest – introduced her to a convent in London. After a one-week retreat there, she told the Mother Superior she wanted to join. The Mother Superior suggested she wait a bit. When Mary was twenty-one, she became a postulant, then a nun.

When she was fifty-one, Sister Mary found she mistrusted her original decision to live 'away from the world'. She became depressed. At the suggestion of the convent's physician, she began four-times-a-week psychoanalysis. My invoice was paid each month by a cheque, signed by her Mother Superior.

Sister Mary did not find it easy to talk to me about sex. She'd had a long-term sexual relationship with another nun – 'I tell her what I want her to do.' On another occasion, she told me her Order restricted conversation to specific times of the day, and that it was forbidden to prefer the company of one nun over another. Consequently, she regularly had to confess to 'breaking the silence' and having 'a special friend'.

After two years of psychoanalysis, Sister Mary left the convent. She joined a support group that helps former nuns move back into the secular world. Through this group, she met and began to date Patrick, a former priest.

Two months before their wedding, Mary and Patrick began to argue about sex. Mary told me she loved the intensity and pleasure of their sexual relationship, but she found herself delaying the start of penetrative sex. She'd now agreed to have intercourse on their wedding night but was frightened that when the time came, she wouldn't be able to go through with it. 'It's not the sex. I'm still anxious about getting pregnant.'

Soon after the start of Sister Mary's psychoanalysis, we discovered she had a near-psychotic fear of pregnancy. 'Can you imagine having a body inside your body?' she asked me. 'It could burst out.'

In the early months of our work together, we were able to map out some of the origins of her phobia. First and foremost, there was the trauma of her pregnant mother's sudden death. But other events in her childhood seem to have contributed to her dread. When she was eleven, her Religious Education class watched an explicit documentary film about 'the miracle of childbirth'. The towels soaked with blood and the tiny baby covered in afterbirth caused Mary to faint. Another memory came to her: when she was thirteen, Niamh, her best friend, was killed by a drunk driver while riding her bike home. Mary described Niamh's funeral, Niamh's mother calling her daughter's name over and over again. 'She couldn't stop wailing. She lost the run of herself.' From this point on, Mary knew she couldn't be a mother – she was terrified of her yet-to-be baby's birth and death. Having a baby, she believed, would kill her.

Bit by bit, we came to the view that Mary became a nun to avoid pregnancy, and now – having gone through the menopause – something in her had changed. She was ready to leave the convent and re-join the world.

In the weeks leading up to her wedding, we discussed the re-emergence of her fear of pregnancy, and as we did so, her anxieties about intercourse faded away. Later, describing her wedding night, Mary told me it was 'a healing. It left me feeling rooted and lifted.'

4

When you were a small child – vulnerable, full of need – what did you learn about intimacy?

Mary learned that sex led to pregnancy, which can be fatal. It was only after the menopause, and two years of psychoanalysis, that she felt safe enough to leave her convent and begin to have intercourse with a man. In other words, a dread of pregnancy structured her sex life.

Abigail absorbed the fact that she was unlovable, a painful truth that was reinforced daily by the way her father treated her. Her feelings of longing for her remote father and her feelings of hate were buried so deep in her that she thought she'd rid herself of them. But those undetectable feelings gathered together and became a mighty unseen force directing her sexual behaviour.

How we think is who we are. Years later – after Abigail had married, become a mother and achieved some success as an academic – when we were coming to the end of her psychoanalysis, she told me that the realisation that she was incessantly talking to her father in her mind was a turning point. She began to think about him and herself differently. 'As he decreased in size, I had more room in my head for my own life.'

Matt learned that hate ruins everything. His sexual life was his solution to the problem of not feeling free to hate the person he loves. Because he always had to be 'nice', he was always in motion – moving between Jemima and various other sexual partners. This activity helped him reduce the risk of feeling hate towards her. (An affair, masturbation, sex workers – all of these can be used to keep aspects of oneself from one's partner.) Matt had organised his life so that his animosity could be split-off and directed away from those he loved. His work as a political consultant allowed him to hate those at a distance, his political enemies. Because he could not express his hate, his closest relationships felt artificial and shallow – to use his word, 'unreal'.

These patients came to me in various states of despair. Love, too, can cause us to feel vulnerable and helpless. Maybe it is only in this state of mind – when we are unsure of what to do, when we no longer know which way to go – that we are motivated to understand ourselves better.

We can only make sense of our sexual selves if we travel towards ourselves. This inward expedition leads us back and forth through time. As we remember, we discover. Discovering, we remember. Knowledge of our heart must come from our heart. We don't receive this knowledge. We find it at the end of a journey no one else can make for us.

Connections

1

I first met Susan Wolff and Cora Siskin in July 1990, when I began attending a small biennial conference of American and European psychoanalysts. Over six years, at four meetings – Cork (1990), Copenhagen (1992), Antibes (1994) and Glasgow (1996) – I got to know the Wolffs, Susan and her husband Paul, and the Siskins, Cora and her husband Martin. I was in my early forties, unmarried, and I attended all of these conferences alone.

It was in Cork that I first noticed Susan. We were in the same clinical seminar. Her hair loose, in long dark curls, with little or no make-up, she reminded me of my undergraduate days at Berkeley. I warmed to her Americanness: she touched people when she talked; she smiled when she said hello to the hotel staff.

Every seminar at this conference was made up of eight people – four psychoanalysts from America, four from Europe. We represented different psychoanalytic societies, different clinical traditions. The aim was for each of us to learn how the others worked. The procedure was simple: each participant presented work from an anonymised, ongoing analysis – recount the patient's life history, give a description of the psychoanalysis, and then, read aloud a 'he-said, I-said' account of a recent session for the group to discuss. Slowing the clinical process down in this way reveals the nuts and bolts – the relation between the analyst's theory and practice.

Because her flight was delayed, Cora missed the first presentation but she joined our group after lunch. She wore a navy suit, and her blonde hair was tied back in a neat bun. Her reserve made her appear a bit old-fashioned, so her clinical presentation came as a surprise.

Cora took her place in the speaker's chair. She handed out a copy of the session she was going to present, set her copy aside, leaned forward, and began to speak. She described her work with a man in his thirties, whom she called John Smith. This patient was successful, intelligent and obliging, but he was unable to form any meaningful attachments, though he hardly realised it. He drifted from woman to woman. He had a kind of equanimity, reasonableness, but this pseudo-maturity was achieved at the cost of all real emotional contact with himself and others. Cora said she felt he was 'uninhabited'. She had an eloquence.

In the session she read out, Mr Smith talked about his girlfriend ending it with him, in his usual abstracted way. Cora was silent. Eventually, she said, 'So when do you think I can meet John?' The patient's mind was jumbled. She let him stay that way for a while. Then she said, 'You're talking to me as if we're colleagues – two psychoanalysts discussing a patient – someone named John Smith. If I'm going to help him,' she went on, 'I need him to come into this room, to bring his worries to me.' Then, after a long pause, she added: 'We're talking *about* John, I need to talk *to* John.' The effect on the patient was electric.

During the discussion, an alliance began to form between Susan, Cora and me. Most of the group were absorbed in a conversation about Mr Smith's diagnosis. Was he on the spectrum? A hysteric? The three of us were interested in the feel of the session: how he kept his distance, and why. Susan made the point that there are patients, diverse in their psychopathology, who present with one common feature: they give a performance of being a patient. How, she asked, can we reach a patient who will not bring himself into the analysis?

That evening, we all gathered in the small hotel restaurant. I met Susan's husband, Paul, a food journalist and cookbook author. As I write this now, I remember him in a black polo jumper and pleated khaki trousers. Born and raised in New York, he was big, open, direct. He talked to me about their three teenage children, and his never-ending struggle to lose weight. Straightaway, I liked him.

Cora's husband, Martin, was also there. Though he was a psychoanalyst and taught in the Department of Psychiatry at NYU, he was not participating in the conference. When I asked him how he was spending his time, he told me he wasn't doing much – reading, hiking a section of the south coast; he'd also hired a ghillie for a day's fly-fishing on the River Lee. Martin struck me as kind-hearted, and yet no-nonsense. I thought he was probably a first-rate psychoanalyst.

Both the Wolffs and the Siskins were from New York. Susan and her husband had recently bought a brownstone in Brooklyn. Cora and her husband lived with their two teenaged daughters on the Upper West Side. Although Susan and Cora had much in common, they trained at different institutes, were members of different psychoanalytic societies and had entirely different styles.

Before dinner, Susan had been for a walk along the coast. She came into the restaurant in a lightweight waterproof jacket and old but well-cared-for leather hiking boots. She carried a canvas tote. There was something relaxed, even free-spirited about Susan. When Cora arrived for dinner, she wore a black suit with white shirt. Her manicured nails were dark red. Although Cora was warm, welcoming, she looked like she'd come from a business meeting, though this couldn't actually be the case.

The Wolffs and the Siskins were appealing people. I'd lived in England for over a decade, but I was American, and I missed the States. Looking back, I can see now that I was attracted to each of them as individuals, but I was also drawn to their Americanness – their self-confidence, sense of anticipation and belief in the pursuit of their happiness.

In 1992, the participants from Cork were invited to Copenhagen for the next American–European clinical conference. Once again, each seminar was made up of eight people – four analysts from America, four from Europe. In keeping with the purpose of the conference – to learn how psychoanalysts from other traditions work – Susan, Cora and I were put in different seminars. When we could – coffee breaks, meals – we sought each other out. After hours, we did stuff together. I can't remember what we talked about. I know we spent whatever time we could together.

Two years later, at a conference in Antibes, I ran into Susan in the hotel lobby on the first night, the night before her clinical presentation. She was concerned, she said, that her presentation wasn't very good. Could I go over it?

Her patient was difficult – a depressed, self-destructive twenty-three-year-old woman, entangled with her mother. Susan's patient seemed to want the psychoanalysis to fail, and so did her mother. In one exchange, Susan gently explained to the patient that she might want to make a mess of her psychoanalysis to reassure herself, and her mother, that the only person able to help her was her mother. The patient began to cry, an opening for Susan to talk to her about the sadness of growing up.

Susan's clinical work was excellent, and I told her so. Again, she started to tell me she was disappointed in herself. She stopped. She had the alertness to recognise that her sense of failure might be related to her patient. 'She's a perfectionist,' Susan said, 'she may want to see how I cope when things go wrong.' Her insight impressed me. As she wrote a note to herself, she said, 'I must remember to make the point that my failure might have value. It can be useful to watch your psychoanalyst accept her limitations, admit failure.' Susan gave me a hug.

We found the others at a bar across the street from the conference hotel. Paul was telling the Siskins about his brother. He'd had cystic fibrosis and died when he was eleven. Paul described the positive effect of his brother's life, and his enduring love for him. That night, each of us spoke about our childhoods, our parents, our lives. I told them about the woman I'd recently broken up with. Cora asked me what I was looking for in a wife. 'Someone who'll be good in a divorce,' I said.

Everyone laughed. I told them I wasn't joking. 'I want someone who in the worst possible situation will be the best possible person: fair-minded, kind.' I couldn't imagine having this easy conversation with my English colleagues.

The Wolffs and the Siskins were roughly ten years older than I was, and I looked up to them. I was sort of in love with them as couples. I admired their marriages and hoped for something like that for myself.

On our last night in Antibes, we skipped the organised event. Instead, we wandered around the old town, ending up at a tiny hotel-restaurant that Paul had found. After dinner, we moved outside to drink and continue talking. At some point, well after midnight, I went back into the near-empty dining room to ask the maître d' if he would order us a taxi. As he telephoned, I waited. From the bottom of the garden, through the tall open doors, came the sound of Susan, Cora and Martin laughing at something Paul had said. I remember feeling tipsy, happy, lucky to know them.

All this was several years before email became the common way for people to stay in contact with one another. We rarely telephoned or faxed, we didn't meet up between conferences, and yet, after six years, we were at home with one another. The five of us had become friends.

2

Then came the Glasgow conference.

On the first morning of the conference, a Saturday, I found Susan in the hotel lobby inspecting the seating plan for that evening's 'gala dinner'. She looked up and saw Martin. 'Why aren't we together?' she asked him.

Martin looked at her blankly. 'If you want to know why, ask your husband.'

Susan went to her hotel room to find Paul. Paul told her that for the past two years – since the previous conference in Antibes – he'd been having an affair with Cora.

Susan stormed out. She found Cora and Martin's hotel room. Cora was there alone. Voices were raised. Susan told Cora that they needed to talk. Two hours later, at a café a few streets away from the hotel, they met.

That night, neither Martin Siskin nor the Wolffs attended the gala dinner, but Cora and I did – she said she needed to get out of the room and she wanted to talk. She had not meant for Susan to find out on this trip, or in this way, she said. She didn't tell me how

Martin had found out, and I was reluctant to ask. Cora spent most of our conversation rehashing that day's argument with Susan, going over and over what they had said to each other. The next day, Sunday morning, Susan gave me her version. It was practically identical to Cora's.

And then the conference was over. On Sunday evening, I took the train from Glasgow to London. For most of the five-hour journey, I found myself staring out the window, playing and replaying their conversation in my mind. At some point, after dark, I did what I tend to do when I'm at a loss. I opened my notebook and wrote it all down.

3

Susan was already at a table, with a cup of coffee, wearing sunglasses, when Cora walked into the café.

('Straight out of Barthes,' Cora told me later. When I asked her what she meant, she reminded me of that section in *A Lover's Discourse,* titled 'Dark Glasses', which describes the hurt lover's attempt to be both admirable and pitiable – wearing dark glasses both to hide *and* to draw attention to his red-eyed distress.)

Susan's opening startled Cora.

'You don't teach or publish much. I thought you were into your family.'

Cora said nothing. Then she said, 'Susan, you asked me to meet you here. I'm here.'

'What is the matter with you?'

'Nothing's the matter.'

'No – something is *seriously* the matter with you. Getting old? Death?'

Cora answered calmly. 'I don't know what – exactly – you want me to do here.'

'I want you to stop fucking my husband,' Susan said.

'Not going to happen.'

'*What?*'

'That's not going to happen. I'm not doing this to attack you. I'm doing this because I want to build a life with Paul.'

'You *want*? Hitler *wanted* Poland.'

'Stop.'

'That's exactly what *you* should do – *stop*. Stop with the manicures, the red nail polish, the designer suits – stop fucking my husband, and get some marital therapy.'

'I'm here because *you* said we needed to speak.'

'We're speaking, but *you're* not listening. Turn on your receiver.'

'I'm listening, I've heard you. I'm sorry you're suffering. But there is nothing I can do.'

'Really?'

'It's *your* unhappiness – *your* suffering – *you'll* have to understand it, work through—'

'What about the children, *their* suffering?'

'They're not infants. Rachel will be at university in a year. Yes, it will upset the children, but—'

'*Upset?* This is a catastrophe for my children – and yours.'

'Let me finish! Yes, it will *upset* the children – all of them – but in time, they might learn something valuable from all this.'

'What on earth can your pathetic midlife crisis teach my children? Don't fall in love? Don't get married?'

'Know what you want. When you find it, go after it.'

'You sound like a fridge magnet. My children don't want stupid slogans. They want their mother and father together.'

'Life doesn't end just because we have children.'

'Actually, you're wrong there. When you have children, you don't get to do whatever the fuck you want. Get over yourself. Why don't you and Martin get help? Fix your marriage – instead of wrecking mine? You're an analyst, for Christ's sake.'

'I know that.'

'Then *grow-the-fuck-up!* I'm sorry you never learned what being a psychoanalyst is really about – so I'll tell you: mending. Repairing. Having empathy. Caring for others. Respecting boundaries. Seeing reality. Not stealing a friend's husband. *Being fucking moral*. Why are you laughing?'

'I don't know what I'm laughing at – maybe it's you. You don't sound like a psychoanalyst. You sound like some old rabbi. Your nineteenth-century notion of being "grown-up" – by which you really mean I should behave. That's not my idea of psychoanalysis.'

'Trying to break up a married couple? Steal a daddy from mommy? You're a mess. How can you pretend to help anyone when you run your life like this? What does Morrie say?'

'I'm sorry?'

'Have you gone back into analysis?'

'I don't need to go back to Morrie.'

'Oh Cora, you really, *really* do need to go back to Morrie.'

'I know what he'd say.'

'He'd tell you to stop acting like a slut and start acting like a psychoanalyst.'

'No. He'd say: "You don't want to hurt the people you love, but if you have to hurt them to become yourself, to have the life you desire – then that's what you'll do."'

'For one minute, can you think like a psychoanalyst actually would?'

'That's what I'm doing.'

'No, you need to start thinking that maybe what you really want – *really want* – isn't Paul, but to fuck up those who love you.'

'I didn't do this to hurt my family...'

'And yet that's *precisely* what you're doing.'

'I'm sorry for the pain I'm causing my family, and you. I am. I truly am. But this isn't a tragedy. It's not some terrible biopsy. No one is going to die. We're all going to survive this. It's just life.'

'There's no point in talking to you.'

'Susan.'

'You're so sure of yourself, so sure of the future.'

'Of course, I don't know the future. But I want a future with Paul. That makes more sense to me – and him.'

'Don't talk to me about what Paul wants. You're a sociopath.'

'You're being ridiculous. I'm human.'

'This is going nowhere.'

'Well, I think we got somewhere. We got all this out in the open.'

'Go fuck yourself.'

Susan pushed herself away from the table.

'Don't leave,' Cora said.

'I hate you. Martin hates you. Your daughters, my children – they're all going to hate you. And one day – because you've fucked up his life – Paul will hate you.'

Susan continued speaking as she stood up: 'Try to understand that.'

She reached into her canvas tote bag, took out her wallet, slapped a five-pound note on the table, and walked away.

4

Alone with each other at the gala dinner on that last night in Glasgow, Cora and I found an empty table. Over gristly roast pork and mashed swede, she told me the story of her affair with Paul.

'A month after Antibes, after the August break, when we were back in New York, I rang him. I asked Paul if he would like to meet. He said yes.'

'That was a big step.'

'Our last night in Antibes, during the taxi ride back to the hotel, I rested my leg against his. He didn't move away. When all of us were saying goodnight, I could feel he didn't want me to go.'

'And then?'

'We met for a coffee. He told me he liked what I was wearing. I told him that I'd dressed for him. We walked out of the café, he took my hand, led me into an alleyway, and we kissed. That was it.'

After the waiter filled our wine glasses, she continued.

'I loved him for being honest – not telling me that he didn't get along with Susan, or that they were thinking of separating, or that he was lonely. Once I asked him if they were unhappy.'

'And?'

'He said, "Of course not."'

Cora folded her napkin. 'I'm not,' she said, 'someone who believes you can only love one person.'

It upset her to hurt those she loved, especially the children. 'It would have been easier if we could just have carried on having an affair, but we fell in love. I can't say it any other way.'

Cora was silent for a moment, and then she looked up. 'I can tell you this: the intimacy I feel with Paul is something I've never had before.'

'So, it's the sex?' I said, teasing.

'Yes, partly,' Cora said, laughing. 'I always thought I was a sexual person but, actually, I've never had a great sex life, so I could never be sure.' She continued, 'Up until now, I used sex as a means to an end: the way to get a man to love me. The way to make up after a fight. The way to keep a marriage ticking over.'

Cora laughed again. 'Psychoanalysts treat sex as a variable in the couple equation, a quantity that can be adjusted. It's more than that. Good sex isn't tricks, it's magic. It changes how you feel about yourself, the world.

'On so many levels, sex with Paul has changed me. I always had a hard time being myself. I have more courage now. I engage with people differently. I connect. I feel I'm fully myself. At fifty-six, that's a miracle.'

'That sounds wonderful.'

Cora looked away. 'I can't even begin to... It makes me cry. I can't even begin to describe what that feels like because the level of connection I feel with Paul has transformed me.'

'You can cry, it's all right.'

'I'm okay,' Cora said. 'It's not a bad cry. I'm crying from happiness, relief – that I found Paul, that he found me. He sees me. I see him.'

Using her napkin, Cora wiped her tears. We decided to move from the dining room to the hotel's bar. Sitting in a quiet corner, drinking whisky, Cora gave me a detailed account of her exchange in the café with Susan.

'Do you remember Cork?' Cora said.

'Yes,' I said, 'why?'

'Do you remember the patient I presented – Mr Smith?'

'The one you called "uninhabited".'

'That was me,' she said. 'What I mean is that I understood that patient because I was a lot like him. Martin is a lot like that too. It was the marriage we made together. There was plenty of order, harmony, good meals, family celebrations – champagne, happiness. But we both left a lot of ourselves outside our marriage. We never fully connected with each other. We tried – we *really* did – but we've never been able to change that.'

The next day, Sunday morning, Susan rang my room at 8.30 a.m. She asked me if I'd like to go with her to the Burrell Collection. We didn't walk around the galleries, we sat outside, drank iced tea, and talked – she worried about the children, raged at Paul, grieved about their lost future.

After putting the five-pound note on the table, she'd gone back to the conference centre to try again to talk to Paul. He told her that he didn't want to separate, but he was not going to give up his relationship with Cora. They'd shouted. He cried. She cried. At some point, after midnight, he went to bed. Susan was too agitated to sleep, 'I thought, "Dying can't be worse than this."' Susan realised it was still early enough to call New York. She rang her best friend, then dialled her old psychoanalyst. Nothing either of them said had eased her pain. How could it? And yet, Susan told me, 'There was a moment, the sun was already up, when I stopped going over and over everything. I felt, for a minute or two relieved.'

'Because you now know the truth?' I asked.

'Not just that,' she said. 'I thought, "This is who I'm going to be: the wife who's been left, the single mom, the psychoanalyst. Okay, I can do this. I can do this."'

For a few minutes, we sat in silence. Then Susan asked me what I was thinking.

I told her I'd remembered something she'd once said – was it in Copenhagen? We were talking about marriage. Nothing had prepared her for the strength of her feelings, she'd told me. 'You know how we teach our students that where there's love, there's hate? Sometimes, I hate Paul so much, I'll be washing the dishes, then I'll turn around and there he is, and I am genuinely surprised he hasn't vaporised.' At the time, we laughed.

'I remember,' she said. She smiled, and then her eyes filled with tears.

5

A year later, I was in Glasgow again, this time to give a talk. I hadn't been back to the city since the conflict erupted between Susan and Cora.

The train home, from Glasgow to London, was late. It was after midnight when I arrived at Euston Station. I closed the book I was reading, gathered my things from the overhead rack, and walked to the Underground. Between Camden Town and Chalk Farm, the Northern Line lost power. For ten minutes, the train sat in a tunnel. There was no sound but the rustle of a newspaper, and the rhythmic murmur from a young man's headphones.

When I got home to my flat, I unpacked, took a shower and went to bed. I was exhausted, but I couldn't sleep. After a while, I got up, made a cup of herbal tea, then found my notebook from the previous year. Sitting at the kitchen table, I read through Susan and Cora's exchange again.

One year on, their argument still disturbed me. Not as a moral issue – who was I to judge? I felt their row was about something more than Cora's affair with Susan's husband; more than Cora's desire versus Susan's helpless rage. These were two esteemed psychoanalysts, in a desperate moment, using psychoanalytic concepts as sword and shield – scrapping with each other about the aim of psychoanalysis.

Susan's belief, as I saw it, was that psychoanalysis aims to help the patient accept reality – to 'grow up', as she put it. Our lives are connected, interdependent. Because insight leads to a more truthful perception of ourselves and others, psychoanalysis is therapeutic: we hurt ourselves and others less. To Susan, Cora wasn't thinking like a psychoanalyst, because she was being impulsive. Her affair had nothing to do with love. Her desire was annihilating. Susan's position might be boiled down to: what's good for the pike is death for the minnow.

For Cora, a psychoanalysis ought to reveal us to ourselves – expose our desires in all their complexity, contradiction and ambivalence. Her position came down to: take what you want, and pay for it. A psychoanalysis, she seemed to be saying, should aim to free the patient's mind so that – as long as she's prepared to accept the consequences – she can act. Life is short. Stay, leave: everything has a cost.

Susan's view fit with my training, but Cora's resolve to live her life was compelling. Shouldn't *this* be the aim of psychoanalysis – to help my patient become herself?

I flipped from one position to another. I thought about my patients, and my own psychoanalysis. Plainly, each psychoanalysis will have many different aims: small practical goals (arranging when to meet, for example) and outcome goals (reducing anxiety, say). There are immediate goals (making sense of some piece of behaviour) and life goals (choosing a partner or career). But beyond these various aims, what is *the* aim of a psychoanalysis?

I took a sheet of white paper from the drawer and began to put down phrases:

The aim of a psychoanalysis:
— to make what is unconscious, conscious (FREUD)
— to increase the patient's capacity for work and love (FREUD)
— to help the patient let go of neurotic suffering and embrace the misery of everyday life (FREUD)

A new phrase seemed to arrive every few minutes, rooted in the memory of a seminar, a supervision, a conversation, a bit of reading. I felt as though I could continue writing for hours.

— to break the spell of self-deception (AMADEO LIMENTANI)
— to gain insight – only insight leads to the reintegration of lost parts of the ego, allowing for growth (HANNA SEGAL)
— to tolerate ambivalent feelings and experience the world with less fear and fragmentation (MELANIE KLEIN)
— to heal the wound of early trauma (MICHAEL BALINT)

CONNECTIONS

- to see early trauma not as a wound to be healed but a door to growth (MICHAEL EIGEN)
- to escape the illusion that we must either control or be controlled (JESSICA BENJAMIN)
- to impart an awareness of death – it is this awareness that liberates us from neurotic fear (NORMAN O. BROWN)
- to accept absence; to live without false assurances or a false identity (OCTAVE MANNONI)
- to think about our thoughts rather than act on them impulsively (MICHAEL FELDMAN)
- to wrest knowledge from suffering (JONATHAN LEAR)
- to hear the patient's emotional truth, not give them some formulaic interpretation (DINORA PINES)
- to make room for 'the yell of joy'; to provide a place where it is safe to be creative (MARION MILNER)
- to show the patient the limits of my understanding (DONALD WINNICOTT)
- to see the unseen; cast a beam of intense darkness so as to see what has been obscured by the glare of illumination (WILFRED BION)
- to restore to the patient the freedom to be uninteresting (JANET MALCOLM)
- to let the unconscious speak so that it can heal itself (CHRISTOPHER BOLLAS)
- to accept there is no cure, no possibility of wholeness (JACQUES LACAN)

> — to be ourselves, or more accurately, *become* ourselves
> (THOMAS OGDEN)

I had listed maybe twenty such descriptions when I saw the paradox. Yes, of course, a psychoanalysis should do all these things – just as it should help a patient accept reality (Susan) and live her own life (Cora) – but not by *aiming* to do so.

An aim is an intrusion on the patient's autonomy – an attack on the power to identify one's own desires, decide one's own mind. Guiding the patient, even towards some benefit, limits psychoanalysis. Over time, as Freud gained clinical experience, he became alert to this danger. In paper after paper – especially in the *New Introductory Lectures* – he set out his view that a desire to cure the patient, what he called 'therapeutic zeal', is a sign of the psychoanalyst's underlying cruelty. 'Helping the patient', 'improving her well-being' – these aims can disguise an unconscious wish to limit the patient's freedom.

And now, looking over my list, considering carefully the difference between 'helping' and 'understanding', I think of something the psychoanalyst Wilfred Bion once told a patient: 'I don't know why you're so angry with me – I'm not trying to help you.'

6

After the Glasgow conference, I didn't hear much from Susan, Paul, Cora or Martin. For a few years, every once in a while, I would get a message from Susan on my answering machine. Would I see a former patient who had moved to London? Could her son, who was coming to England, ring me? The daughter of a friend was struggling; did I know a good psychotherapist in Edinburgh? But at some point, Susan's calls stopped. I remember seeing Martin once more at an international psychoanalytic conference in Rome. He smiled at me from across a room, and then he turned to talk to someone else.

In 1998, two years after the Glasgow conference, I received a photograph in the post. Cora and Paul were sitting side by side in a New York subway car, dressed-up, smiling. On the back, Cora had written, 'On our way to City Hall to tie the knot!' I sent them a note of congratulations. After that, I don't remember hearing anything from Cora. We were friendly, but no longer friends.

After Glasgow, a friendship with any of them wasn't possible. Our lives had moved in different directions. I married, had children. Though I felt a sense of loss, I can't say I thought badly of any of them. I missed our friendship.

7

Our story has one more beat.

Twelve years after Glasgow, in April 2008, I was in New York to visit family. I received an email from Paul. 'Dear Friends,' it began. 'Early Friday morning, after I left our apartment, Cora fell in the bathroom, and hit her head.'

When he'd returned home at lunchtime, she was still breathing. Cora was taken to hospital. She was brain dead. Until her daughters could get back to New York, she was kept on a respirator. On Sunday morning, with Cora's daughters present, the respirator was turned off.

As is the Jewish custom, the family sat Shiva, which meant a week of mourning at home. Paul's email invited everyone to come.

When I arrived, the front door was open. The apartment was overflowing with friends.

I nudged my way down the hall into the warmly lit living room. A scrum of people – the children and grandchildren of Susan and Cora – surrounded Paul and Martin.

'Does everyone have a prayer book?' the rabbi said over the tumult. 'We're going to begin.'

Shoulder-to-shoulder, the families formed a circle around the rabbi. Some put their arms around each other, others held hands. The rabbi began to sing the prayers.

A young woman, recognisably Cora's daughter, stood between Paul and Martin. She began to sob.

Paul lowered his head. A woman standing behind Paul placed a hand on his shoulder. He pressed his cheek against her fingers and kissed her hand. It was Susan, his ex-wife.

The moment has become emblematic in my mind.

From time to time in my clinical practice, I see individuals who are legally but not psychologically married to their partners, unable to think of themselves as part of a couple. They rarely speak of 'we'. They may be in a marriage for decades, but they are wedded to something else, typically their work. Or, for another example, I have a patient whose husband drinks. The drink, not their relationship, consoles him. He's legally wedded to her, but psychologically married to alcohol.

The intentions we bring to our romantic relationships are as complex and varied as the goals of an analysis. Nonetheless, I'm convinced that the ability to think of oneself as part of a couple is a developmental achievement. To be properly married one must recognise a contradictory nature: accept oneself and one's beloved as both generous and frustrating, inventive and ordinary, loving and cruel. Crucially, we must try to let go of the restricted and restricting storylines we impose on ourselves and our partners.

This developmental step is not stable. It is forever under threat from our desires. In a heartbeat, we can find ourselves acting like an aggrieved child. When this happens, work is required to re-find ourselves, and our partners. Susan and Paul had loved, hated, married and divorced. But even at this difficult moment, they were still a couple, still doing love's labour.

The Gift

When I was in my mid-thirties, I had a falling-out with my sister. I was training to be a psychoanalyst at the time and having analysis myself. It was my psychoanalyst who pointed out to me that the birthday gift I had just sent my sister – a pair of vintage, Georg Jensen earrings, 'unworn, still in their original box' – was unkind. ('Sadistic' was the word he used.) I objected. I was trying to show my sister that I still wanted to be in touch. 'Haven't you already done that by continuing to telephone and write to her?' he asked.

I'd just finished telling him that my birthday gift to her was 'perfect', that she would love the simple silver earrings. In this way, he pointed out, I'd chosen a gift that would create a problem for her. The gift allowed me to feel better about myself – wasn't I thoughtful? – and then, when my sister didn't respond, or replied in some stiff way, to think less of her.

My outraged protests were proof enough that my psychoanalyst was right. Gift-giving is sometimes a way for nice people to be cruel.

Some years ago, a patient of mine who'd just started his first job as a museum curator was given a new VW Golf by his well-to-do parents. On his salary, he could not afford the petrol, parking and insurance costs, let alone the annual maintenance charges. Selling the car would make his parents furious with him, but keeping the car meant having to ask them for regular financial help, at the very time he was trying to become financially independent. 'I would have been much happier with a bike, but if I tell them that, they'll get angry and tell me I'm ungrateful.'

Recently, an eighteen-year-old patient of mine, Melanie D., was offered a place at Trinity Dublin to study English. This offer was conditional on her obtaining an A grade in her three A level examination subjects: English Literature, French and History. A few weeks before the start of her exams, a week before her Easter break, her parents announced a surprise: as a reward to her for working so hard, they had organised a family holiday in Ibiza over the break. Melanie reminded her mother that she had told her she was on a carefully organised schedule. She had planned on revising during the Easter holiday and, further, she had told her mother that she wanted to go on holiday *after* her exams. Nevertheless, her mother shouted at her, told her she was ruining the holiday and called her 'spoiled'.

I thought I had a good understanding of how gift-giving can be used to control, and undermine, but recently I failed to recognise a similar situation.

When Helen T. was six years old, her mother died of a brain

tumour. Her father's work required him to travel frequently between London and various cities on the continent. Unable to cope with his job and look after her, her father sent Helen to live with his widowed mother-in-law. Over time, he visited Helen less and less often. When Helen was eleven years old, he remarried and started a new family. Helen and her grandmother rarely spoke of him. If Helen brought him up, she was 'being tiresome'. As a result of this brusqueness, and her grandmother's rules about what a child could and could not do, Helen learned to be quiet, biddable, hiding her loneliness, grief and depression.

Just after she turned forty, Helen was diagnosed with breast cancer. She'd had surgery and radiation, and now, at fifty-one, she was in good health, though she remained frightened that her cancer would return.

Helen was married with two daughters. She loved to organise lavish family gatherings – for birthdays, New Year's Eve and especially Christmas. She spent all year preparing for Christmas – collecting small gifts for the stockings, wrapping every present carefully, thoughtfully, with each recipient in mind.

I had the impression that Helen did all of this because she wanted her children to have the home she'd never had. But about a year into her psychoanalysis, something happened to make me re-examine this view.

One Monday, Helen began her session by telling me that she'd had a terrible weekend. It had been her birthday. On Saturday, her daughters had insisted on making her a big birthday lunch.

'They really shouldn't have,' Helen said, sounding put out. 'They're both busy – they have their own lives. And we were going out with friends for dinner.'

And then her husband's gift had annoyed her. Some months earlier, she'd seen an antique pearl necklace in a West End jewellery shop, and her husband had bought it for her as a surprise.

'He must have thought you liked it,' I said.

'He says I told him I loved it.'

'Did you?' I asked.

'I don't know – probably. But I didn't think he'd buy it – it was very expensive.'

'Your husband isn't careless with money.'

'He was really angry with my reaction.'

'What did you say to him?' I asked.

'I thanked him, and...'

'And?'

'And later, I asked him if we could return it. I told him I didn't really like it – it's just too much.'

Helen liked telling me about the gifts she gave, but not the gifts she received. The birthday lunch her daughters had prepared had bothered her ('they're always so messy in the kitchen'). And why had her husband booked dinner for later that evening if he'd known there would be this lunch?

Something similar occurred in her sessions. Whenever our conversation gave Helen some relief, something seemed to happen in her – rather than feel thankful, she got irritable. She'd find something wrong with what I had just said – I should have told her my idea earlier, why had I waited so long? Or, wasn't I just saying something her friends had been telling her for a long time?

When I tried to talk to her about her lack of appreciation – 'You don't seem to be very grateful for your husband's efforts' – she refused to think about it. 'But the necklace really is too expensive,' she insisted.

The day after this exchange, Helen came in looking unsettled. She'd had a nightmare. 'There were two spiral staircases side by side,' she said. 'I was going up one and my mother was coming down the other. I reached out to touch her, but she was just out of reach.'

As she told me the dream, Helen gestured – drawing with her fingers two staircases in the air – and then she remembered something. Towards the end of her mother's life, when her mother was very weak, Helen would sit on the edge of her bed and her mother would do her hair for school. 'I loved her plaiting my hair; she loved doing it,' Helen told me. 'She could do French plaits, weave ribbons into my braids. I loved the feel of her hands, stroking my hair.'

'Your mum loved you. She loved taking care of you, giving to you. You felt grateful to her.'

Helen covered her face with her hands.

Helen longed to be closer to her husband and daughters, and yet, unconsciously, she was frightened of the depression she suffered when her mother died – and for this reason, she sought to avoid feeling grateful.

Gratitude roots us in reality. To be grateful to someone is to recognise that we've received something good from them. It makes them real to us. While Helen did not give gifts to be unkind or sadistic, she did want them to be so perfect that they would eclipse any she received. She gave gifts to protect herself from feelings of gratitude.

Sparks

I had my first glimpse of life as a psychoanalyst when I was a student at Oxford. After graduating from Berkeley, unsure what I wanted to do next, I went to Oxford to study Philosophy, Politics and Economics. It was 1976 and, at the time, psychoanalytic theory wasn't taught in any department. Most Oxford academics considered it 'pseudo-science'.

But psychoanalytic theory made sense to me. More importantly, reading Freud, Klein and Winnicott helped me make sense of myself, so I joined the University of Oxford Psychoanalytic Society. Our small student society of about ten members was essentially a reading group – we met to parse a psychoanalytic text, and sometimes invited a working psychoanalyst to present a paper.

On a bright morning in May, a few days before the end of term, all ten members of the group piled into the back of a rented windowless van to make the four-hour, 175-mile trip to the seaside town of Southwold for a seminar with Anna Freud.

To the members of our small student group, this meeting was momentous.

At the time, Anna Freud, who was Sigmund Freud's daughter, was the most famous living psychoanalyst. She had been his colleague, confidante and, in the end, his nurse. Anna Freud was also the founder of child psychoanalysis and a distinguished psychological theoretician herself. Not just Freud's biological heir, she was, to many, his clinical and theoretical heir – a sort of psychoanalytic head of state.

The gathering was hosted by Dr Marie Battle Singer, one of a small number of women psychoanalysts who all had weekend cottages in or near Walberswick. In her invitation, Dr Singer had proposed we arrive at her home on the Saturday at 11 a.m. We would have coffee, and then Miss Freud and her lifelong friend, the psychoanalyst Mrs Dorothy Burlingham, would drive over to Southwold for our meeting. The seminar would run from 11.30 to 1 p.m. Dr Singer promised to give us some lunch before our drive back to Oxford. Miss Freud suggested to Dr Singer that we discuss her book, *Normality and Pathology in Childhood*.

In the days before our meeting, I imagined the seminar with Miss Freud: at the start, formal, ceremonious; then, becoming relaxed, intellectually exhilarating, consequential. There'd be sparks – quick-thinking, astute disagreement. She'd be impressed by our knowledge and understanding. Invigorated by the discussion, reassured for the future of psychoanalysis, she'd take our student society under her wing. She'd conclude the seminar with an invitation to continue our discussion at her home in London – not next month, next week. I imagined her taking a particular liking to me.

We were in awe of everything about Miss Freud: her Viennese accent; her dark, sad eyes; her distracting resemblance to her father. Like acolytes meeting their high priest, we were suddenly self-conscious. We came ready to discuss her book; she seemed vaguely surprised by this. She was distant, reluctant to reply to our questions. When Ingo, a German student doing his doctorate in mathematics, asked, provocatively, if all theories of psychological development imposed an unfair notion of 'normal' development, she looked at her hands, smiled, then shook her head no. Nothing we said would draw her out. Mrs Burlingham also hardly spoke. Perhaps their reserve was intended to create a space in which we might speak freely, but the effect was the opposite. By withholding their immense intellectual and emotional knowledge, their absence created a black hole that sucked all the light out of the room. About an hour into the seminar, I looked over and saw Ingo, legs crossed, now foot-tapping, as he silently read the titles of the books in Dr Singer's bookcase. By the end of the seminar, I felt empty.

Later we gathered for iced tea in Dr Singer's garden. Dr Singer made sure Miss Freud and Mrs Burlingham were comfortably settled in the shade, then brought each of them a glass. I was taking around a bowl of crisps when Miss Freud waved me over. Standing close to her, I sensed something flowery, a soap, perhaps Floris, Lily of the Valley. After confirming that I was the group's president-elect, she said: 'Did you know that in the twenties and thirties, during my father's time, there was a student group like yours at the University of Vienna?' I was so startled by the realisation that Anna Freud was talking to me about her father that I couldn't respond. She brought up Bruno Bettelheim, 'He's director of the Orthogenic School for Disturbed Children at the University of Chicago – Ernst Kris too, both were members of that group. He edited my father's papers, and brought psychoanalysis to Yale.' She looked into my eyes and smiled. 'You never know,' she said, 'from little groups like yours, great things can grow.'

It was only then that I saw that Miss Freud had most likely agreed to this meeting not because she wanted to discuss her book, but because she was committed to the cause – *für die Sache*, as her father put it – disseminating psychoanalytic ideas. She wanted psychoanalysis on the curriculum at Oxford. I hoped she would become our teacher; she wanted us to be her vanguard. When the seminar began, Miss Freud seemed to me empathetic, wise. Now, she still had these qualities, but I felt she was somewhat rehearsed. My exchange with her, the realisation that she had probably mentioned her father because she knew the effect it would have on me – and that she'd undoubtedly made this move countless times before – left me even more disenchanted.

After she and Mrs Burlingham had spoken to all the members of our group, they got in their car for the short drive back to their cottage in Walberswick. As they drove off, we waved goodbye. I was going back inside, feeling vaguely disappointed about the day, when Dr Singer asked if I would help her clear away the glasses, and bring out lunch.

It was only at this point – after Miss Freud had left – that I properly saw her colleague, Dr Singer. Child psychoanalysts of that time often dressed like children themselves: no jewellery, a plain smock or apron-like dress – Miss Freud had had that look. Marie – as she was insisting I call her – was stylish: a bright yellow blouse, a colourful Liberty silk scarf around her neck; her thick hair was brushed back, shaped to frame her face. Marie was Black, and in her early sixties – all the psychoanalysts I'd met thus far were White, and seemed significantly older. I was curious – Marie's accent wasn't British, but I couldn't place it. She had energy. She also had a warmth.

Marie's house was appealing too. It had an airy, simple feel – more like a contemporary art gallery than an English country cottage: white walls, dark, wide oak floorboards; in the sitting room, a kilim on the floor and another across the sofa; in the centre of the wall, above the sofa, there was a small, intense, abstract oil painting.

In the galley kitchen, on the counter next to the stove, was a glass Chemex coffeemaker. Almost everyone I knew in Berkeley or New York had one, but I'd never seen one in England. Then I saw a large platter of fried chicken and a bowl of potato salad on the counter. I asked Marie where she was from.

'I'm from the States,' she said. 'But I've lived here a long time.'

Speaking with almost no trace of an American accent, she told me she was from the South, and had grown up in Mississippi. She'd graduated from Boston University, then studied social work at Smith College. After the war, she came to Europe, first to Germany to work with displaced, unaccompanied children, then to London, to train with Miss Freud.

Marie and I carried the food, plates and drink into her garden; everyone helped themselves. Sitting kitty-corner at one end of the picnic table, we ate, and continued to talk. I see her turning in her chair to look at me, as we spoke – I remember her telling me more about her teaching in Cambridge. When she saw a small book in my coat pocket, she asked me about it. I showed it to her and in response to more questions I told her what I knew about the author (Tranströmer was a psychologist in a boys' prison) and what I liked (the poems' quiet, contemplative feeling). She opened the book and read the first poem to herself, then read it again out loud to me:

2 A.M.: moonlight. The train has stopped
out in a field. Far-off sparks of light from a town,
flickering coldly on the horizon.

As when a man goes so deep into his dream
he will never remember that he was there
when he returns again to his room.

Or when a person goes so deep into a sickness
that his days all become some flickering sparks, a swarm,
feeble and cold on the horizon...

She took out a small pad, made a note of the author's name and the title of the book.

About Chekhov, Gorky once wrote that in his presence 'everyone felt an unconscious desire to be simpler, more truthful, more himself'. Marie was like that. Her way of being had undone my disappointment with the seminar. My emptiness was gone. In its place, I felt a desire to be more straightforward, more myself.

After we'd finished clearing away the dishes, she told me she needed my help in the sitting room. Once inside, she said she wanted to roll up the carpet.

'You're students, aren't you? I thought you all might like to dance.'

On the floor next to her bookcase was a phonograph, and a stack of records. She took an LP out of its slip cover and carefully placed the record on the turntable. Billie Holiday's wistful voice filled the room.

'Let's dance,' she said.

The doors of the sitting room were wide open and the music flowed out into the garden. Soon, all ten members of the University of Oxford Psychoanalytic Society were inside, dancing or swaying in small groups.

At some point, as we danced to Ella Fitzgerald and Louis Armstrong singing 'They Can't Take that Away From Me', she said: 'They tried to psychoanalyse the dance out of me. Couldn't take *that* away from me.'

When it was time to go, Marie said, 'Now, don't you *ever* let them analyse the dance out of you.' Then, she took my hand.

Although we never met again, Marie had shown me more than what I wanted to be – she'd shown me a way of being.

Love and Time

When I first met Osman M. for a consultation, I couldn't make sense of his quiet equanimity. Given the events of his childhood, the challenges he was describing, the tall, elegantly dressed man sitting opposite me should have been unsettled in himself. Instead, he spoke calmly, and with great insight.

Four months after he was born, Osman's parents left Eritrea, and emigrated to England. Osman was left behind in the care of his grandparents – his mother's father and mother. Once they were settled in London, they planned to return and collect him. That never happened.

When I asked Osman to tell me about his grandparents, he recalled waiting for his grandfather to come home from the hospital where he worked as a surgeon. Osman described the excitement, his anticipation, as he looked out the window, waiting to announce his grandfather's arrival. His grandmother would change her dress and put on lipstick. Then, while she made dinner, Osman and his grandfather would sit on the floor in the dining room and make things together – a model of their home, for example, with small pieces of wood, glue and plasticine.

When Osman was nine, his grandfather died of pancreatic cancer. Two years later, his grandmother was killed by a motorbike. A few days after her death, without explanation, Osman was taken to Asmara airport, to start the first leg of his journey to England.

Arriving in Stockwell, Osman discovered that his parents were divorced. His mother had remarried, and he had four half-siblings, all under the age of six. On that first day in London, he was taught how to use an iron, then given three baskets of ironing to do before he could go to bed. From the age of eleven, until he left for university, his mother and stepfather treated him as a servant. Remembering this period – his confounding grief, loneliness – Osman described waking in the night to the smell of his grandmother's cooking, and on other occasions, waking with a start because he heard his grandfather calling his name.

Osman loved school. He spent as much time as he could there. He became especially close to his chemistry teacher, Mr Harris, and to the headmistress, Ms Fry. When he was eighteen, he was offered a place to study medicine at St Bartholomew's Hospital. After training as a doctor, he became a psychiatrist, and in time, a child psychiatrist. He worked in Camden with some extremely difficult adolescents. This was how he came to be in my office. He now wanted to train as a psychoanalyst, and he wanted me to be his training analyst.

A few months after his psychoanalysis began, Osman told me

that he'd discovered that his girlfriend of four years, Tara, had been sleeping with her boss. When he told her that he had decided to end things with her, she threatened suicide. Tara was a barista-turned-model-turned-paralegal. While clearly an attractive woman, she suffered from a profound fear of abandonment. From time to time, so he couldn't go to work, she hid Osman's mobile phone, wallet and keys. On one occasion, when Osman was to deliver a paper in Paris, she hid his passport. She could suddenly become mocking, bitter. She lashed out, and even hit Osman. Her inability to manage her emotions made me think she might have a personality disorder.

Two months after they broke up, they got back together. This was their pattern. In the years before Osman's psychoanalysis, and in the first two years of our work together, Osman and Tara would be together for several months, then break up. During their break-ups, they texted each other but did not see each other. Then they'd get back together. One reason was sex. Incredible, he said. The best sex he had ever had. 'Surely our sexual chemistry means something?' he asked me. Another reason was his conviction – an omnipotent belief, it seemed to me – that his love would fix Tara. I pointed out that no matter how much time or love he gave Tara, she was unchanged. 'I don't give up on people,' he said.

When Osman was not in a relationship with Tara, he dated other women. Though he told me he was eager to meet 'the right woman', he avoided women who were colleagues, or in any way his intellectual peers. He didn't date women who were more success-ful than he was. He especially avoided women who were soothing.

Osman was drawn to women who had broken wings, women who were unsettled and unsettling. One of his dates always ordered the most expensive dish on the menu, he told me. I remember thinking: 'All the lobster thermidors in London can't fill that emptiness.' He asked me to recommend a psychotherapist for Tara. He asked me to recommend a psychotherapist for almost every woman he dated.

When he was dating, Osman overwhelmed each woman with extravagant dinners, holidays. 'Falling in love' or being 'in love', as he described it, seemed to be a form of masochism. He was overly attentive to the needs of his partner, but he wouldn't let his partner know his needs, which made it impossible for her to fulfil them.

In his psychoanalysis, he enacted his desire to always be the caregiver. A few months into his psychoanalysis, for example, Osman noticed that I had lost a small amount of weight. (None of my other patients noticed.) 'Have you seen your doctor?' he said. On another occasion, he noticed a bandage on the back of my hand. He asked how I had hurt myself. I was fine, I replied, and yet, the next day, he brought me a small tube of anti-bacterial cream. This judo-throw – Osman helping the person who is there to help him – allowed me to point out to him that he used his capacity to care as a defence against being cared for. In his erotic relations, I added, it was the same: his over-attentiveness was a defence against being attended to.

Osman's over-attentiveness reminded me of my fussy over-conscientiousness in my training analysis: we both were resisting surrender.

In my psychoanalysis with Dr Limentani, I discovered that I loved my parents, but I didn't altogether trust them. This was not really their fault. I was born with a birth defect. Between the ages of two and seven, I had to have a series of surgical procedures. The experience was harrowing. My parents did not know how to deal with what I was going through. They never talked to me about my surgery. I think they believed that if we didn't talk about it, I'd get over it sooner. I became over-conscientious to reassure them that I was okay. I couldn't speak my anger. So began my masquerade of goodness.

Over-attentiveness was Osman's disguise. When speaking about his childhood, Osman was quiet, thoughtful, composed. And yet, listening carefully to Osman's dreams and associations, I came to believe that unbeknownst to himself, he was angry with his parents for leaving him, his grandparents for dying and his mother and stepfather for their cruel treatment. Unconsciously, he seemed to me full of rage, but anxious about hurting those close to him. (When he became angry with someone at the centre of his life, he would bury his anger; then, he'd erupt with disproportionate indignation towards someone at the periphery of his life – a parking attendant or department store salesman, for example.) Seen in this light, his quiet equanimity, the quality I had first noticed in him, looked different. His gentle manner was a way of demonstrating to others – and to himself – that he was empty of dangerous aggression. His excessive care was a way of safeguarding those close to him.

In addition, by always being the caregiver, Osman protected

himself against a particular aspect of surrender – regression to a state of dependence. He wanted his partners to trust and emotionally surrender to him; but, because of the events of his childhood, he dreaded the idea of surrender to someone else. Osman accepted this understanding, and we discussed it at length over many months, but he didn't change. In his words: 'I don't want to be the person I am, but I don't seem to be able to become the person I want to be.'

Then, almost three years after the start of his psychoanalysis – during another period of no contact with Tara, at a time when he was dating various women – a shift occurred.

Osman was telling me about a consultation he'd had that morning with a seven-year-old boy, an Afghan refugee. As he spoke, I heard associations to his own Eritrean childhood. As Osman described a drawing the boy had made for him, a picture of his home in Kandahar, I remembered Osman sitting on the floor with his grandfather, building houses.

I told Osman that I thought he was caring for this boy as his grandfather had cared for him when he was a frightened little boy. 'By doing so,' I said, 'you're continuing your grandfather's life.'

Osman took a long breath. For a while, he didn't speak. Finally, he said he'd never seen it that way. 'I'm thinking about my grandfather, my grandmother – Mr Harris, Ms Fry, my teacher and headmistress – I'm thinking about the people who made me who I am,' he said.

In the quiet that followed, I found myself thinking about

the people who made me, loved me into being. After a while, I found myself thinking about my first stages of becoming a psychoanalyst – meeting Marie Singer, starting my training analysis with Dr Limentani. It was comforting to think I was continuing them, their work.

And then another thought arrived.

One day, in the not-too-distant future, this will all end. In a split second, everything will vanish. That day, fifty years ago, with Marie in Southwold, the first days of my own training psychoanalysis, my image of Osman on the floor with his grandfather – all this thinking – all my thoughts, feelings, will disappear. My way of being, all of it will be gone. Psychoanalysis will continue. Osman and my other, younger colleagues will be in their consulting rooms working with their patients but, soon, I will be no more. No thoughts, no words. Nothing.

Returning from these thoughts, I could now see I'd made a mistake.

Osman was busy looking for the 'right' partner. He thought that his problem was how to find love. His real problem was to accept the fact that one day, he will lose it.

All love comes to an end. Osman didn't want to think about this fact. His on-again, off-again, never-ending relationship with Tara; his hectic dating, the over-attentiveness to a stream of women – who he once told me felt 'interchangeable' – all this giving, and yet, there was, to use his words, 'no forward momentum'. Because love ends, Osman avoided love. Unconsciously, he had constructed a way of being that allowed him to live in the illusion that love has no end.

The great task of love, and also the great task of life, is to see ourselves and others clearly. To see reality, we need something I once saw described as a kind of binocular vision: one lens to see our life, and the other to see our own personal extinction.

Over the years, I had talked to many patients about the distinctions it is possible to make between submissiveness and surrender. In those sessions with Osman I saw something more. I understood when we surrender, we accept our self, the other, and *also* the reality of Time. Love – discovering another person matters to us – anchors us in Time.

I spent some minutes thinking about how I might put these thoughts to Osman. Then I told him that what I had said about his grandfather's life wasn't the whole truth.

'What's the rest?' he said.

'The rest is this: your grandfather is dead. I will die. One day, you will die too.'

Osman tensed. 'I know that. Probably better than you; I'm a medical doctor.'

'I'm not thinking of some patient dying on a ward, or death in general,' I said. 'I'm thinking about my personal extinction, and yours.'

'I don't see what my death has to do with anything.'

'Love always comes to an end,' I said. 'I think your focus on "meeting the right woman" keeps you from this fact.'

'I don't have a problem with endings – goodness, my grandfather died, my grandmother died. I'm ending things all the time.'

'I think it is *because* of those deaths – you seem to be avoiding an experience of someone ending it with you, or losing someone you love to death.'

'I'm trying,' Osman said. 'I just can't find the right person.'

I reminded Osman that his relationship to Tara was unchanged, that sometimes he felt his girlfriends were interchangeable. 'You've told me that you feel your relationships go nowhere, that there's no development. Maybe that's the point. Maybe the aim of all your dating is to protect you from love.'

I was being unfair, Osman told me. He started to remind me of one of his more successful relationships. They'd been on the verge of moving in together, he'd even considered proposing.

Then slowly, almost imperceptibly, the energy drained from Osman's voice until he stopped speaking altogether. Osman was lying on the couch so I could not see his face, but I thought I heard him struggling not to cry. 'I don't get beyond a certain point,' he said.

A quiet settled in the room. Something had changed.

'We have to find a way to sort this out,' he said.

'Yes,' I said. 'We do.'

When it was time to stop, Osman sat up on the couch, but he did not leave, something he'd never done.

'I just need to sit here a moment,' he said.

Going Home

In August 1987, a few months before I qualified as a psychoanalyst, I returned to Indiana to look after my mother. My parents' house was right on Lake Michigan. In the evenings, despite the heat, my mother liked to open all the windows. She liked the sounds filtering in – bits of conversation from the sidewalk, the neighbour watering his lawn, a distant train whistle. On the days when she was confined to bed, I prepared the macrobiotic foods that she believed were making her better. At night I slept in a reclining chair near her bed, or, if the heat was especially oppressive, on the living-room floor.

At the end of the month, my sister arrived from Santa Barbara to take over, and I returned to London. A few weeks later, during a hospital visit, my mother turned to say something to my sister, then couldn't. She sat upright, gasped for air, and then slumped forward in her chair. My sister shouted for the nurse, who came immediately. Then the room was filled with doctors and nurses, who lifted my mother onto a hospital gurney and shooed my sister out, but my mother was past saving.

Nothing had prepared me for the death of my mother – especially not her fifteen years of cancer. The fact that she had had breast cancer, then lung cancer, then breast cancer on the other side, then a 'spot' on her liver – all of the recurring cycles of diagnosis, treatment and then remission, all of it had only reinforced my childlike conviction that she would never die.

In the weeks after her funeral, I felt desperately tired. I would fall asleep in the evenings immediately after work and spend the weekends on the sofa watching old black-and-white films. I didn't understand that this fatigue was a part of mourning, or a part of my mourning. It was a result of the internal work of accepting a new reality – the heavy-lifting of imagining a new future, one in which my mother wouldn't know what had become of me.

If I was looking forward during this time, I was also looking back at my last days with her. We had spent a lot of the time reading together. I would bring her a cup of tea, pull the recliner up to the bed and open a book, usually a collection of Anton Chekhov's stories I had with me. If she fell asleep while I was reading, I put a bookmark in the pages, and the next day we continued from where we'd left off.

Chekhov's stories took us far away from my mother's sickroom, but they were more than a diversion. Chekhov is an observer, an intelligence, capable of taking us deep into the lives of others. In doing so, he shows us how our feelings for each other, and ourselves, can be contradictory, obscure. There is no problem, no climax, no moral. He is the quiet voice of a friend, telling you something essential.

I remember in particular reading the story 'Gusev', about a very sick soldier travelling home by boat. I remember this one because, while I read, I was made increasingly uneasy by the accumulating details of Gusev's illness.

Unable to leave his hammock, Gusev is tormented by a vague hunger, but he can't make out what he wants. There's a heaviness on his chest, a throbbing in his head, his mouth is so dry it is difficult for him to move his tongue. He dozes, he dreams of taking bread out of an oven, and then, Gusev dies.

We think his death is an ending; we expect the story to conclude. But Chekhov does something remarkable. Gusev dies, his body is sewn up in sailcloth, tied with weights, and tipped into the sea – his life ends. And yet his story continues:

He went rapidly towards the bottom. Did he reach it? It was said to be three miles to the bottom. After sinking sixty or seventy feet, he began moving more and more slowly, swaying rhythmically, as though he were hesitating and, carried along by the current, moved more rapidly sideways than downwards.

Then he was met by a shoal of the fish called harbour pilots. Seeing the dark body the fish stopped as though petrified, and suddenly turned round and disappeared. In less than a minute they flew back swift as an arrow to Gusev, and began zig-zagging round him in the water.

> *After that another dark body appeared. It was a shark. It swam under Gusev with dignity and no show of interest, as though it did not notice him, and sank down upon its back, then it turned belly upwards, basking in the warm, transparent water and languidly opened its jaws with two rows of teeth. The harbour pilots are delighted, they stop to see what will come next. After playing a little with the body the shark nonchalantly puts its jaws under it, cautiously touches it with its teeth, and the sailcloth is rent its full length from head to foot; one of the weights falls out and frightens the harbour pilots, and striking the shark on the ribs goes rapidly to the bottom.*
>
> *Overhead at this time the clouds are massed together on the side where the sun is setting; one cloud like a triumphal arch, another like a lion, a third like a pair of scissors... From behind the clouds a broad, green shaft of light pierces through and stretches to the middle of the sky; a little later another, violet-coloured... The sky turns a soft lilac. Looking at this gorgeous, enchanted sky, at first the ocean scowls, but soon it, too, takes tender, joyous, passionate colours for which it is hard to find a name in human speech.*

After reading, I put the book aside and put a hand on top of my mother's. When she fell asleep, I adjusted the blinds and headed down to the lake.

Sitting in the dune grass, clouds rising overhead, I thought

Gusev's story was not disturbing, quite the contrary. It had seemed to calm my mother, and it had given me more peace than I'd felt all summer.

In the distance, I heard the low steady clickety-clack of a slow train. I sat there listening, waiting for the sound of the whistle. For a moment, everything was still.

Hauntings

1

Near the end of his session, Tobias B., a sculptor, started to describe a dream he'd had – something about coming across a large sculpture on a beach. His telling was so quick, and the dream so slight, that I worried I'd missed most of it.

'I'm sorry, would you tell me that again?' I asked.

Tobias had been coming to see me for about ten years at this point, and in that time had almost never shared a dream. During this decade he had also found it increasingly difficult to make art, though we hadn't spent much time discussing that either.

In the dream, Tobias is on the beach. He finds a large milky white form, a sculpture, about his height, washed up in the sand. Tobias said, 'I thought it was fibreglass, but looking closer, I could see it was more like a crab's shell.'

He turned his hands so his palms faced each other, modelling the air, shaping a small arc.

After a pause he said, 'It was stuck in the sand. The sand was wet and dark and the sea was grey and still. Whatever had lived inside the shell had been washed away.' He added, 'Like an animal had got trapped in the sand and died.'

He folded his hands in his lap.

'That's it, that's the whole dream', he said. 'I'm looking at this washed-up, broken shell, and I have the idea that once this sculpture was a living thing, but now it's dead.'

Tobias looked at me. 'What do you think?'

'Tell me what feels important to you about the dream,' I said.

He wasn't sure. Then he said, 'Stuck – the sculpture was stuck in the sand. It was dead. The dream felt like a nightmare. It woke me up.'

'Do you remember our last session?' I asked.

Tobias looked puzzled.

'I used the word "stuck" – we both did – quite a few times,' I said.

Tobias nodded. 'Oh, yeah.'

'I'm thinking your dream may be a response to that conversation.'

It has happened before that a patient will describe a dream that seems to directly address something I've said during the previous session. A few years ago, I sought the advice of a colleague for one of my cases. This colleague was full of insight. At our next session, I enthusiastically repeated my colleague's ideas in my interpretations to my patient. The next day my patient reported a dream in which he was in a Savile Row tailor's shop. A salesman had him try on several suits. 'They were beautiful, each fit me perfectly,' he said, 'but the experience was kind of creepy because everything was second-hand.'

In a similar way, I thought Tobias's dream might be a response to an idea I had raised in our previous session. I *had* used the word 'stuck' a number of times. The language Tobias used in describing his dream was even more vivid: 'washed-up', 'broken', 'an empty shell', 'a living thing,' that's now 'dead' – these words better described the experience Tobias was having of his life. Tobias's dream also made me feel, in a way that I hadn't before, that I could see, as if through a chink, down, down, for miles beneath my feet, some essential thing, an aspect of Tobias that I hadn't considered. I felt that in telling me his dream, Tobias was unknowingly, unconsciously, telling me that he wasn't just stuck, he was dead.

2

Being 'dead in life' may sound odd, but the phrase accurately describes a number of patients I've seen over the years. The phrase has its roots in the psychoanalytic concept of 'the dead mother', a hypothesis developed by the French psychoanalyst André Green to explain a particular form of emotional deadness. Green is not talking about people who have actually experienced the death of a parent. He is trying to describe patients who were raised by a mother or father who was physically present, but who was, one way or another, emotionally absent, lifeless at a critical time in their child's development. Typically, the dead mother will feed, bathe and change her baby. She will do all the things a mother should do; but, because of some deep preoccupying despair, she cannot be a source of vitality. Green believed that the child of a dead mother, or dead father, could grow into an adult who is positive, energetic, entertaining – but that this animated persona is the after-effect of the child repeatedly trying to revivify the dead parent. Other clinicians have suggested that the child could be mimicking the other parent, the partner who was trying to counteract the lifeless parent. And yet, because of the way we internalise both our mothers and fathers, the deadness gets passed on.

Characteristically, these patients come to me because someone else, usually their spouse, suggests they get help. At the preliminary interview, they rarely mention their inner deadness. Their cold core only emerges over time. Beneath their enthusiasm and charm – their considerable academic or professional accomplishments – there is an almost hallucinatory emptiness they cannot understand. 'I have everything: wife, children, a good life. But at certain moments, I can feel the most crushing desolation. My life seems meaningless,' one patient told me.

Always keen to give a good performance, such patients are often successful sexually – and yet, they cannot love. Their driven, energetic sexualisation is a defence against the deadness, the desolation. The 'love' they give, like the 'love' they once received, is an impersonation of love: very thin milk.

Tobias's deadness was different. It wasn't the result of some problem in his early development, a 'dead' mother or father. His lifelessness began shortly after the death of his girlfriend, Misaki. Of course, the death of a partner causes grief, despair, sometimes depression, but this sort of death-in-life – I'd never seen anything like it. If his psychoanalysis was to be a success, this was a mystery we would have to solve.

When we first met, Tobias was an up-and-coming artist. He'd already appeared in a well-known art magazine's '40 Under 40'; he'd had a small solo exhibition at a major London museum. Galleries and collectors in America, Asia and Europe were buying his work. He had friends, family – a life.

In the ten years I'd been working with Tobias – the decade since Misaki's death – this life had slowly ebbed away. The gallery that represented him went into receivership. He found it difficult to settle in at another gallery. Unable to pay the mortgage on what had been both his studio and his home, he rented out the property. He used the money he received to cover his expenses. To avoid becoming homeless, he became a 'property guardian' – someone who pays a nominal rent to live in a vacant building – but this meant he could be forced to move at any time. Often, he was. Eventually, Tobias took up an offer to live as a property guardian in an empty school, far outside of London, away from friends and family. We continued to meet regularly, but ten years after he began his psychoanalysis, it would be fair to say that Tobias had all but stopped making sculpture. He'd given up any thought of having a relationship, given up on having children. 'I'd be embarrassed to bring anyone back to where I live,' he said.

Throughout this period, I did the things a clinician is supposed to do. I took my work to colleagues for supervision. In time, I sent Tobias to a colleague, and then to another, for further assessment. Their interventions were equally unsuccessful.

There will be long periods in a psychoanalysis when the psychoanalyst's feelings are in agreement with his clinical understanding. But sometimes the emotions roused in him are much nearer to the heart of the matter than his conception of the clinical situation. Sometimes, his unconscious awareness of the patient is a step ahead of his clinical understanding. I thought Tobias was stuck, and I told him so. The following week, speaking to me through his dream, he told me something I'd been feeling for some time, but I had been unable to think, let alone put into words: Tobias was dead.

In the First Elegy of his *Duino Elegies*, Rilke imagines what it is like to be dead:

> *Granted, it's strange to dwell on earth no more,*
> *to cease observing customs barely learned,*
> *not to give roses and other things of such promise*

Death, for Rilke, is not a physical condition, it is a particular state of feeling: the dead *feel* strange because they have no future. It *feels* strange to let go of the past, to 'ignore even one's own name like a broken toy'.

Later he observes:

Strange, not to go on wishing one's wishes. Strange, to see all that was once so interconnected drifting in space.

At some point that I had failed to see, Tobias had stopped desiring his desires. Emptied of desire, he was no longer in the arc of life: birth, growth, death. Disconnected from the living, he was 'drifting in space'.

3

Tobias and Misaki met in April 2008. He was thirty-four, she was twenty-seven. He had been making work for a gallery in Japan and had been spending time in Tokyo. One of his pieces had been chosen for an exhibition of new sculpture at The National Museum of Modern Art in Kyoto. Tobias and Misaki met at the exhibition's opening. 'She stood out, but she was comfortable with it . . . and the way she was dressed . . . she was stylish, cool . . . she was . . . way out of my league, but I went up to her.'

They exchanged phone numbers and arranged to meet. 'Over dinner – it was our second date, I was going back home the next day to visit my parents in Berlin – she suddenly told me, "I know

I don't have to tell you everything, but I want to tell you this. A year ago, I got sick and had to go into a hospital because I was hearing voices. I was very ill, but I got better. I'm fine now." Her honesty was endearing, but because she didn't seem to me to be at all neurotic, this information was surprising.'

After dinner, Misaki volunteered to guide Tobias across Kyoto to his hotel. On the pavement outside his hotel, when they said goodnight, she pulled him close, kissing him passionately, lightly biting his lip. Later, she would tell Tobias that it was the fact that he didn't invite her up to his room, his restraint, that left her feeling he was a man she could trust. Misaki decided to come to London for a month. They had had only two dates.

A few weeks later, several days after arriving in London, Misaki gave up her hotel room and moved into Tobias's home, a studio in the East End where he lived and worked. Tobias did some work during the day, but mostly they spent time together. They went to art openings, dinners and parties.

Soon after moving in, Misaki told Tobias that she wanted to go to Camden Market. In one shop window, she saw shelves of glass pipes and other drug paraphernalia. 'I could see in her face,' Tobias said, 'the place excited her.' Inside, there was a young Japanese man on the till. Misaki got into an animated conversation with him. Afterwards, she told Tobias that she'd asked if he could get her some crystal meth. She said that in Japan they called meth 'the fast one'. The man had told her that it was hard to get crystal meth in England. 'That was the first time I heard Misaki talk about meth,' Tobias told me. 'It was something I didn't know anything about.'

Two days later, while Tobias was at his gallery, Misaki returned to Camden, found someone on the street selling drugs, and bought amphetamines. When Tobias got home, he found her on the bathroom floor, vomiting into the toilet.

They got into an argument. Tobias told Misaki that her drug-taking worried him, and that she couldn't take drugs in his home. 'I remember saying something like, "Please don't make me feel like I'm just your hotel." Then she did this remarkable thing. She burst into tears and told me that she wouldn't do it ever again, and that she'd only done it because she "wanted to keep a distance". She was frightened of falling in love with me.

'After that, I pretty much stopped working to spend time with her because I knew we only had a couple more weeks before she had to return to Japan. And I started thinking about where our relationship was going. If someone lives in the same city, things can move very slowly for quite a long time. You can drift. Whereas if someone's going back to the other side of the world, then you ask yourself – is one of us going to move to the other's country? I don't know if it was because of that, but it certainly happened that we began talking about having children together. That was a conversation I'd never had with previous girlfriends, women that I'd been with for far longer.

'I want you to know things were intense – emotionally, sexually – in every way,' Tobias said. 'Sometimes sex was slow and gentle and we would just stare at each other and kiss for hours. At other times we were like two wild animals, scratching and biting. When she orgasmed, for a moment she looked entirely different. I felt I was seeing her – who she was, who she'd been. I could see deep into her heart. I fell totally in love with her, and she told me that she felt the same. Our relationship was unlike anything either of us had experienced before. We talked intimately about everything. She told me about herself, her problems, her breakdown.'

This breakdown, Misaki told Tobias, had been caused by crystal meth. A university friend had introduced Misaki to meth. While her friend had smoked it only once or twice, Misaki had found it difficult to stop. A year before she met Tobias, she had found herself smoking meth every day. She became increasingly wound-up, sleeping and eating less and less, until she just unravelled. She spent several months in a psychiatric hospital.

Why had Misaki self-medicated with crystal meth? Was it depression? Her way of avoiding love? While I couldn't get a clear picture of her or her inner world, I had the impression that she saw Tobias as her saviour, the man who would rescue her from her problems. But how did Tobias see Misaki? Because her English was limited, she was deeply unknowable to him. This allowed him more space to create her, imagine her into being.

And then there was her attractiveness. 'If she wanted to,' Tobias told me, 'she could turn it on. Her way of dressing, being – she could become a work of art.' On one occasion, Misaki and Tobias invited several friends to tea in the West End. Wanting to make it a special occasion, she put on make-up, a vintage white satin dress, and a new pair of white canvas Chuck Taylors. Travelling across London on the Tube, they boarded a train that was filled with children on their way home from school. The children crowded around Misaki, asking questions, talking to her, taking selfies. Walking up Piccadilly, a group of women tourists asked if they could take a photograph with her too. Many years later, when Tobias told me this story, I felt he wanted me to know that when she wanted to, Misaki could cast a spell, enchanting men, women and children the way she had enchanted him.

Tobias wanted to take Misaki to Berlin to meet his family. But they discovered that she couldn't change her airline ticket. They agreed that she'd go back to Japan for a few weeks, then return to London for an open-ended stay.

When she returned to Japan, Tobias and Misaki spoke on the phone daily. Her first Saturday at home, she told Tobias she was going to a party that evening. After that, her calls stopped. She didn't reply to his calls, texts or emails. Tobias was bewildered, then devastated. 'I thought she was ghosting me,' he said. 'I thought that she'd met someone at the party and dropped me.'

Six weeks later, just when he'd begun to accept that he'd never hear from her again, he got a telephone call. 'It was this very small, timid voice, telling me that she was in hospital, that she was sick.' Later she told Tobias that she'd gone to the party and 'overdone the crystal meth'.

They resumed talking on the telephone every day. Three

months later, just after being released from hospital, Misaki returned to London. Her mother had paid for the open-ended airfare. 'I was wary about her coming back, but I was also happy about the thought of being with her again,' Tobias said.

Long after the last of the passengers from her flight had come through the arrivals hall, Tobias heard his name being called over the public address system; an official voice was asking him to please come to passport control. He was shown to an interrogation room. A Customs and Immigration officer explained that because Misaki was coming into Britain with such a large quantity of anti-psychotic medication, Tobias needed to confirm that she was staying with him, and that he was prepared to look after her. After he agreed, he was taken to another room. Misaki was seated at a table. She'd lost weight. 'She was a shadow,' he said.

Tobias and Misaki quickly settled into a routine. Tobias would work most days, and some evenings. Misaki would stay with him in the studio. Curled up on his daybed, she'd read or listen to music on the headphones Tobias had bought her. When Tobias stopped for a break, they would take a walk or have something to eat. In the evening, they might go to an opening, a film, or meet up with friends for dinner. They both avoided talking about her time in hospital, her breakdown or her crystal meth-taking. Despite this shared disavowal, or perhaps because of it, slowly, Misaki seemed to get better. 'We spent a lot of time just holding each other,' Tobias said. 'There were some good times. Our relationship deepened, but this second stay wasn't easy.'

The medication that her Japanese psychiatrist had prescribed made Misaki sleepy. Tobias was working long hours, preparing work for an upcoming exhibition in Tokyo, and found himself having to look after Misaki too. He was doing the cooking, the cleaning, the laundry. He made sure they spent time outside every day, usually an hour's walk along Regent's Canal. 'After five months of living together, I think she sensed my frustration, because one day she told me that she was returning to Japan. She planned to go out to Tokyo ahead of me, a few weeks before my exhibition opened. Obviously, I worried. I thought there was a pretty serious risk that she'd use crystal meth again. But she said that she had started to hear voices again. They frightened her. She needed to be near to her doctor. I believed her.'

Six weeks later, less than year after they first met, Misaki went back to Japan by herself. She got off the plane, went to her parents' house in Osaka, and found some crystal meth that she'd left hidden there. Shortly after smoking it, she telephoned her mother at work to say that she wasn't feeling well. She asked her mother to come immediately, which she did, but before her mother arrived home, a passer-by rang the police to say that Misaki was standing in the middle of the road, screaming.

It was two weeks before Misaki rang Tobias. When they spoke, she told him that she was in a secure psychiatric unit. 'She knew I was coming, and she wanted to be well so that she could be with me, and we could go away to Bali on holiday together. I thought she was getting better. Her psychiatrists thought she was getting better too, so they'd decided to transfer her from the secure unit to a psychiatric ward with a rehab centre, in an ordinary hospital.'

On her first day in the new hospital, Tobias and Misaki spoke again. She was quiet, reflective. 'I was firm with her. She was more herself. She told me that when I got to Japan, I could visit her there because she had told the staff I was her fiancé. She might even be able to come out and stay with me in my hotel. She said she missed me. She told me that she loved me. I told her I loved her. When I hung up, I felt calmer. I even felt hopeful.'

The next morning, Tobias told me, Misaki left the hospital and walked several blocks to a high-rise apartment building she had lived in as a child. A few weeks later, Tobias was shown the building's CCTV footage: Misaki takes the lift to the roof garden. 'You can see her sitting on a bench, listening to music on the headphones I gave her,' he told me. 'After about half an hour, she walks to the railing, climbs over and disappears.'

'You're telling me that she committed suicide,' I said.

'Well, whether that was all deliberate and she got...' Tobias trailed off. 'Or whether she even knew what was happening, it is very unclear. She walks to the edge and just keeps going. She doesn't hesitate. I don't feel it was a considered decision in any way.'

'Are you saying you think she was on drugs, crystal meth?' I asked.

'No, no she wasn't on drugs – I mean she was on the drugs her psychiatrist had given her. I was thinking it was more an accident.'

'You don't think it was suicide?'

'The night before, she told me that she had given up cigarettes,' he said. 'Who gives up smoking, if they're planning on killing themselves?'

I didn't answer. I couldn't answer. I had a feeling of overwhelming sadness for Misaki and for Tobias. I found myself thinking that Misaki giving up smoking is *precisely* the sort of thing someone on the verge of suicide might do. I remembered a story a colleague told me about a patient who had attempted suicide by swallowing 200 aspirin. She took 199, and then wouldn't swallow the last one, as it had fallen on the floor and might have germs on it. Suicide is an intensely ambivalent act. The desire to die must overcome our will to live. As I write this, I remember another patient, a young woman, whose father cut his wrists. The coroner's report described a series of 'hesitation marks' on his forearms – the little cuts he made before he threw himself into the difficult work of self-murder. Tobias was clinging to that small part of Misaki that wanted to live, refusing to see the larger part of her that went to the top of a tall building determined to destroy herself.

Another thing struck me: the way Misaki had raised the hopes of her psychiatrists and Tobias, convincing them that she was getting better. This is not unusual in the pre-suicidal patient. Whatever its cause – a feature of her own escalating internal conflict, or a driven, sadistic desire to hurt – by raising their hopes, Misaki had left her psychiatrists, and Tobias, with a heightened sense of confusion, failure and remorse.

'It never occurred to me that she would die,' Tobias said. 'I don't think it ever occurred to me that our relationship could end.'

4

The week after Tobias told me his dream, he arrived for his session early. He appeared different in some way that I could not immediately recognise. His energy was different too.

As soon as he was seated, he said, 'I recognise the sculpture – the milky white form – I know what it is.'

Tobias leaned forward. 'Two weeks after Misaki's death, I went out to Japan, to Osaka. I met with her sisters and mother. Her dad didn't want to see me. I wanted to tell him that I tried to look after her,' Tobias said, 'that I did my best.'

He continued, his voice sharper, determined. 'After I got to their house, the four of us went into their living room to sit near this memorial, a shrine to Misaki – photographs of her, flowers, incense. We talked for a while. Small talk.

'Then Misaki's older sister asked me if I would like to see Misaki's bones. Her English wasn't very good. I assumed she meant Misaki's ashes. To be polite, I said yes. Then she took the lid off this box, and there were Misaki's bones.'

Tobias opened his mouth as if to speak, stopped, then tried again. His voice was low. 'They were arranged, folded into this box, with her skull on top, so that when I looked inside it was the first thing I saw.'

He went on. 'Her teeth. I recognised them.' His voice began to tremble. 'I can't explain the feeling that came over me. I've never felt anything like it. Everything froze. The world stood still.

'She seemed to be smiling at me. I don't know how else to describe it. I thought that Misaki was looking at me, from one side. Except there was another side looking at me as well, because her skull was in pieces. She looked like a Picasso. Then, in the moment after everything had stopped, this thing happened. I assume it is some kind of coping mechanism. In my head, I heard myself say: "Oh Misaki, you're really not looking so good today – what do you say we give it a rest, take it easy for a while?"

'I don't know anyone else who has seen the skull of someone they love. It's just not in our culture. I didn't know it was a part of Japanese culture. I didn't expect it.'

Tobias looked down, then up at me. 'I realised almost immediately after our last session that the sculpture in my dream – *that milky white form* – is the piece of Misaki's skull, the top of her skull, the part that I first saw when I looked into the box. My dream sculpture is her skull.'

He let out a long breath. 'Here I am, ten years later, dreaming about that moment. I can't un-see it.'

Tobias later told me that the Japanese cremate the body at a low temperature so that the flesh is turned to ash, but the bones remain. After the cremation, a Buddhist priest breaks the skull into several pieces. Then, using special, large chopsticks, the family and the priest place the bones in a box, with the feet at the bottom, the skull on top.

'It was more than just seeing her bones,' Tobias said, 'it was the whole thing. Misaki's mother carried her in her womb. And there she was, sitting next to this box with her daughter's bones in it. I couldn't... can't... get my mind around that. And then her mother did something...'

Tobias suddenly looked tired, and I understood that he wanted to tell me more but was struggling.

'Take your time,' I said.

Tobias took a breath. 'At one point during her second visit, one of the sweetest things that happened with Misaki was we went to a concert. We were having a wonderful evening. And she said to me, "Oh, we should get a pair of chains to both wear because we get along pretty good." She said this in her funny way of speaking English and I wasn't sure what she meant. Suddenly, she became very shy. She'd revealed her feelings to me, something she wasn't in the habit of doing. I was moved, and I said, "Of course." Later, she told me that in Japan, that's what some people do when they're getting married; they don't exchange rings, they exchange a necklace that is worn underneath their clothing. Her saying to me, "Let's do this," was her way of saying we should get engaged. So we chose two chains to wear, and we wore them.

'After her sister showed me Misaki's bones, her mother left the room and returned with two bags. In the first was Misaki's chain. It was covered in dried blood. It was covered in her blood from...

because her mother had taken it off her body, when she identified her. She handed that to me... I still have it in the bag with dried blood on it. And then she said, "Here are your headphones." She gave me the Bluetooth headphones I'd given Misaki. So there was this second bag with these broken noise-cancelling headphones – also covered in dried blood. Then, as I was holding these things, her mother said – in a sort of matter-of-fact way – "While the fall crushed her body, her face wasn't too bad, so I had no difficulty identifying her."'

Tobias looked past me, into the middle distance. 'Seeing Misaki's bones, the dried blood on her necklace and headphones – literally to see her blood on things I'd given her. We were there in their living room, talking politely, calmly, but my mind was bursting. I felt sorry about my part in Misaki's death. There's no question, I did. But everything her mother did, it was almost like her saying – I'm sure it wasn't meant this way – but it was as if she was saying, "Look what you've done to my beautiful daughter. She's nothing but this pile of bones." During that visit, I went from feeling sad to feeling like a murderer. Like I killed her.'

As he spoke, I realised for the first time that Tobias had suffered two shattering blows – first Misaki's suicide and then this meeting.

'You're not a murderer,' I said.

'I never, never, should have let her go back to Japan without me,' Tobias said. He began to cry. 'If I had kept her from going home, she would still be alive,' he said through tears.

'Maybe,' I replied. 'Maybe if her mother had collected her from the airport, or maybe if one of her sisters had been waiting for her at home, so that Misaki didn't return to an empty house. Maybe if her father had visited her in hospital, she wouldn't have felt so alone. Maybe if her psychiatrists hadn't released her from a secure ward.'

Tobias wiped his eyes and shook his head. 'I'm sure that's why I never told you about this meeting. I just couldn't. I feel too guilty.'

'You're not responsible for Misaki's death.'

'You don't know everything,' he said. 'In our last call, I told you that I was *firm* with Misaki – that isn't true. I told her that she'd lost so much by taking crystal meth. I said...' Tobias paused. 'I said something snarky. I said, "I hope it was worth it." I told her, "We've lost the holiday we were going to have in Bali. We've even lost the chance to be together in Japan." And she said, "No, no – it's okay, you can come to see me. Family is allowed to come into the hospital, and you're my fiancé." And I told her, "I'm not your fiancé."'

Tobias shook his head. 'I *really* wish I hadn't said that, I *really* wish... She was on a psychiatric ward. That was a terrible, terrible thing to do. To take that away from her. But I was so angry. I even thought my talking to her like that might help her to stop using meth.'

I reminded Tobias that Misaki's crystal meth-taking occurred when she was away from him in Japan, not when she was with him – that coming to England had probably extended her life.

'I hear you, but I feel guilty.'

Tobias's first reaction to hearing that Misaki had jumped from a building and died had been disbelief. He told me that he had felt 'numb, but strangely calm'. He went ahead with the evening he had planned. He had dinner with friends. He didn't feel guilty. His feelings had changed after his visit to Misaki's family. This is not uncommon. Most people react to the suicide of someone they love with disbelief, numbness, denial. Then, a story takes hold: someone is to blame. Family and friends blame the psychiatrist, the ex-husband, someone. People blame themselves. People who know nothing else about Sylvia Plath believe Ted Hughes was responsible for her suicide. After a suicide, perhaps as a way of avoiding feelings of guilt, we find someone to blame.

'I don't think you're responsible for Misaki's death,' I said. 'I don't think her family or doctors are responsible for her death. I don't even think Misaki is responsible for her death.'

'How can you say that?' Tobias said.

'If, by some miracle, she had survived, there is a good chance she would have told you that she regretted jumping. Most survivors of suicide regret trying to kill themselves. I don't think anyone is responsible for Misaki's death.'

'But I *feel r*esponsible.'

'I know, but feeling something doesn't make it true,' I said.

It was this, I thought, his guilt, that was keeping him in a state of protracted mourning, unable to let her go. Tobias once told me that he'd 'lost' Misaki to suicide, but 'lost' can be a very misleading word. He'd known Misaki less than a year, and yet more than a decade after her death she seemed to be constantly in his thoughts. In her absence, she was more present than she was when alive. Death by suicide is unlike any other death: the violence of the act makes mourning – in particular, the letting go – difficult, if not impossible.

One of my first patients, Dr Sarah A., was a junior doctor I was treating for depression. Her father died when she was just four years old. She was told it was a heart attack. In fact, he had cut his wrists. She learned this when she was twenty-five, by overhearing her mother tell a friend she worried Sarah might 'top herself, like her father'. Although Dr A. had few memories of her father, she described his death to me as 'emotionally indigestible'. 'I can't understand it. I can't metabolise it. I can't break it down, absorb it. It is a dense lump stuck in my heart.'

I also had a patient, Mrs Zala B., a cleaner, whose sixteen-year-old son had thrown himself in front of a Tube train. A good student, he left on his desk his carefully prepared GCSE revision timetable, a list of things he wanted for his seventeenth birthday and a handwritten note telling his parents not to worry, that he was now at peace. Mrs B. told me, 'I feel he left in the middle of a conversation. All day, every day, I talk to him.'

5

It had taken ten years for Tobias to tell me that he had seen Misaki's bones, confess to me the feelings he had during that meeting with her sisters and mother. Buried beneath his genuine worries about making a living and having a home, we had discovered a vast underground reservoir of guilt.

Over the next two years, in almost every session, with his dream as our starting point, we explored the sources of this guilt. Why, Tobias asked himself, did I always go along with her? Why didn't I take her to rehab? Why didn't I telephone her parents before she flew home to say she's a meth addict who cannot be trusted to be on her own? Regret, remorse, sorrow – as we located and identified Tobias's feelings, his disposition towards himself slowly changed.

During these months and years of self-interrogation, Tobias would often talk about his dream with a kind of energy that suggested he was not yet finished with it. Before the dream, Tobias had been absorbed in his external world – his difficulties in selling his work, paying his mortgage, finding a place to live, and so forth – now, he was increasingly inward-looking.

Then, more than two years after first describing the dream, Tobias made another confession: 'I shouldn't have put my hand on her skull, I shouldn't have done that.'

'You did that?'

'I picked up her skull.'

How was it that he hadn't told me this before?

A sob burst out of his throat. 'I shouldn't have – I shouldn't have touched her bones, should I?'

I did not reply.

After a moment, he said, 'Her sister was picking up pieces of her skull, almost playing with them, holding them. And she said, "Oh, just bones." I think she was trying to be kind... reassure me. But I could *see* Misaki. When you make love, you're so close. I knew her teeth, the shape of each one, the gaps between them. There they were. The teeth that bit my lip. Unchanged. I never imagined I'd see them again.'

Tobias looked down. 'I think I just wanted to touch her. Comfort her. So I reached into the box as her sister had done. I put my hands on her head' – he corrected himself – 'her skull. And I picked it up.'

At this point, he raised his hands, shaping a small arc, precisely as he had when he initially told me his dream. 'It made this very light, weightless noise, squeaking – an empty sound.'

I pictured Tobias lifting Misaki's skull, holding it – and I had the thought that what he felt was that her skull did not touch him back. He was touching her, but she was no longer there. What was touching him back was nothingness. I told Tobias this.

'I shouldn't have touched her bones,' he said.

He looked down at his lap, then at me. He spoke carefully. 'When I touched her, I caught something. Her death came into me.'

Then he cried, in a way I had never seen him cry.

In the minutes that followed, time slowed down. The moment seemed to expand, becoming a quiet, unbounded space. My thoughts wandered away from the sitting room in Osaka. I found myself in a funeral home in northern Indiana, my mother's service, the moment before we closed her casket. I remembered leaning over to kiss her cheek, and I understood, in a way that I hadn't before, that it wasn't the *coldness* of her skin, it was her *unresponsiveness* that told me she was gone.

Then, not for the first time, I was standing on the dark sand of Tobias's dream. In front of me, the still sea, the sculpture. And I saw that the form – this once living, now dead thing – was *both* Tobias and Misaki. His dream symbolised, embodied, this unspeakable memory: the moment her death came into him.

As I write this, three years have passed. Tobias no longer talks about his dream. It has disappeared from our conversation. 'I'm in a very different place now. Things can still feel hard, but nothing like as hard as they once were,' he said recently. And later, in that same session, he said, 'There are so many things I did wrong, so many things Misaki did wrong too – but why blame her? Or myself? I thought there were some things I would never forgive, but I do.'

I now think of Tobias's dream as a sort of doorway to the underworld. To understand his here and now, we had to descend into his there and then, and to spend time with the dead. My job is to find – in my patients' words, memories, dreams – a way down. A journey to the underworld is a necessary part of every psychoanalysis: to see the light, you have to go down into the dark.

Epilogue: Love and Happiness

Some years ago, I took a holiday with my wife and two kids in Norway. On our first day, we took a hike up a steep mountain path and stopped at an old barn that had once been surrounded by farmland. A few goats and sheep had been brought to graze but the outbuildings were deserted and the barn now housed a small café. A woman made cocoa for the children and tea for us.

The next day, we decided to hike further up the mountain to a waterfall. It was not a particularly good day for a hike; it had rained all night, and the sky was lined with heavy clouds. The footpath was slippery – not dangerous but requiring care. A number of roughly carved walking sticks had been left by the gate for hikers to use, and the children spent some time choosing their favourites.

We were united – as we so rarely are in our everyday life – by our sense of purpose; all quite happy to be walking up the mountain together. The children – they were six and nine years old at the time – were proud to be able to climb so high. Rounding a bend, we came to a small clearing; we took it in turns to lie down in the grass and drink from a stream. Throughout our walk, we had been accompanied by the sound of water running down the mountain as the snows melted. As we approached our destination, this sound became a roar. The waterfall was beautiful, and we were glad to have reached it – to feel how far we'd come.

Sitting on a large flat rock near the falls, we looked at the map, ate Ritz crackers, and took turns taking photos. A few hundred metres above us, the mountains were still buried under snow; the Geirangerfjord stretched below us. My wife and I were struck by the panorama, and the children were too, though they preferred to keep their focus small. My daughter crouched down to pick a flower shaped like a bell, while my son filled his pockets with stones.

As we made our way back down the mountain, I found myself thinking about the way time was passing as we walked – how strange it was to perceive the day unfolding in the expanse of nature, away from my usual routines, and away from other people. I was thinking too about the orderly passing of time in the course of my work. Most weeks, I see the same patient four or five times, often at the same time of day, in the same room, for a set duration. The repetition in this schedule tends to reveal certain small repetitive behaviours in my patients. One patient always arrives a few minutes late. Another never closes the door to my consulting room when she leaves. Another lies down on the couch and cracks his knuckles before speaking. One patient comes into the consulting room and, no matter how quickly or slowly I move to

EPILOGUE: LOVE AND HAPPINESS

my chair, always sits down on the couch at the exact moment that I sit down; this woman was, for many years, a ballet dancer, in the *corps de ballet*. What does this mean? Why would she still wish to synchronise her movements with another's?

What is astonishing about each of these repetitions is that they would be impossible to carry out intentionally. If you made a conscious resolution to misplace your car keys before your weekly visit to your mother – it would be a struggle. But for the unconscious, it is not.

For the psychoanalyst, these habits can be meaningful. The patient who is always a few minutes late, for example, might find it uncomfortable to be early and to sit in the waiting room before his session – he might be avoiding feelings of exclusion. The dancer? She seemed to feel more comfortable, safer, if we were doing the same thing at the same time; it seemed to mean to her that our thoughts were in harmony too.

We all have an investment in these habits of mind. Habit, as Proust pointed out, is 'that second nature which prevents us from knowing the first'. Our small repetitive behaviours might give us a sense of dominion, a feeling that we are in charge of time rather than being swept along in it – protecting us from the experience of time passing, with its feelings of change and loss.

I looked up and saw that I had fallen behind. My family were now some way down the footpath and had almost reached the farm. It was odd to watch them like this, together, but from a distance – my wife in front making sure that no one fell, my son trying to walk along the edge of the path, and my daughter, not putting a foot wrong.

Then I was overtaken by the thought: 'This is how it will be. They'll go on without you; you'll have to let them walk on ahead. You'll be okay – and they will too.'

In the consulting room, I'm focused on details, on the singular aspects of each patient's life. But there, in the mountains, where time is amplified, I felt the connections across the generations. I felt momentarily sad. Then another feeling arrived: the sweetness of desiring what you have – a definition of happiness.

Sources and Notes

Author's Note

The stories in this book are drawn from my work as a psychoanalyst. To preserve my patients' confidentiality, I have changed names and all identifying particulars. If possible, I obtained my patient's permission to use material from his or her psychoanalysis. I am grateful to the patients who gave me permission to publish these reports of our work together.

Portraits of the psychoanalysts Amadeo Limentani, Anna Freud, Dorothy Burlingham, Marie Battle Singer, Harold Stewart and Mervin Glasser are drawn from memory.

Epigraph

Extract from *The Bell* by Iris Murdoch (London: Vintage, 2004). Copyright © Iris Murdoch 1973. Reprinted by permission of The Random House Group Ltd., except in the US and Canada where it is reproduced with permission of Curtis Brown Group Ltd., London on behalf of the Beneficiaries of The Estate of Iris Murdoch.

Prologue: Surrender

Emmanuel Ghent, 'Masochism, Submission, Surrender: Masochism as a perversion of surrender', *Contemporary Psychoanalysis*, 1990,

26 (I):108–36. This essay is also available in *The Collected Papers of Emmanuel Ghent: Heart Melts Forward*, Victoria Demos and Adrienne Harris (eds.) (London: Routledge, 2018), pp. 77–105.

M. Glasser, P. King, M. Laufer, and A. Hayman, 'Obituary: Adam Limentani 1913–1994', *International Journal of Psychoanalysis*, 1995, 76: 1031–4.

Iris Murdoch, 'The Sublime and the Good', in *Existentialists and Mystics: Writings on Philosophy and Literature*, Peter Conradi (ed.) (New York: The Penguin Press, 1998), p. 215.

Martha C. Nussbaum, *Love's Knowledge: Essays on Philosophy and Literature* (Oxford: Oxford University Press, 1990).

Marry Me

Stanley Cavell, *Pursuits of Happiness: The Hollywood Comedy of Remarriage* (Cambridge, Mass., and London, England: Harvard University Press, 1981).

Sigmund Freud (1900), 'The Psychology of the Dream-Processes', in *The Standard Edition of the Complete Psychological Works of Sigmund Freud, Volume V (1900–1901): The Interpretation of Dreams* (London: The Hogarth Press and the Institute of Psychoanalysis, 1953), p. 515.

Phyllis Rose, *Parallel Lives: Five Victorian Marriages* (London: Chatto & Windus, 1984).

John Steiner, 'The Recovery of Parts of the Self Lost Through Projective Identification: The Role of Mourning', in *Psychic Retreats: Pathological Organizations in Psychotic, Neurotic and Borderline Patients* (London: Routledge, 1993), pp. 54–63.

Arthur Valenstein, 'On Attachment to Painful Feelings and the Negative Therapeutic Reaction', *Psychoanalytic Study of the Child*, 1973, 28: 365–92.

Judith Viorst, *Necessary Losses*, (New York: The Free Press, 2002).

SOURCES AND NOTES

Lost Love

Melanie Klein, *Envy and Gratitude: A Study of Unconscious Sources* (London: Tavistock Press, 1957).

Czesław Miłosz, 'Love', from *New and Collected Poems 1931-2001* (London: Penguin Books, 2001). Copyright © Czesław Miłosz 1988, 1991, 1995, 2001. Reprinted by permission of Penguin Books Ltd. in the UK, and in the US and Canada reprinted from *New and Collected Poems: 1931-2001* by Czesław Miłosz (New York: Ecco, 2001). Copyright © 1988, 1991, 1995, 2001 by Czesław Miłosz Royalties, Inc. Used by permission of HarperCollins Publishers.

Philip Roth, *The Human Stain* (London: Vintage, 2001). The phrase 'the ecstasy of sanctimony' is on page 2.

Priscilla Roth, and Alessandra Lemma (eds), *Envy and Gratitude Revisited* (London: Karnac, 2008).

Ignês Sodré, 'Even now, now very now . . .', in *Imaginary Existences* (London: Routledge, 2008), pp. 200-15. An essay on Othello's delusional jealousy, and Iago's envy - the best paper I know on envy and the hatred of love.

Harold Stewart, *Psychic Experience and Problems of Technique* (London: Routledge, 1992).

An Impossible Desire

Christopher Bollas, *Free Association* (London: Icon Books, 2002).

Ronald Britton, 'The Missing Link: Parental sexuality in the Oedipus complex', in *The Oedipus Complex Today: Clinical Implications*, R. Britton, M. Feldman, E. O'Shaughnessy, (eds) (London: H. Karnac Books Ltd, 1989), pp. 83-101.

Sigmund Freud (1914), 'Remembering, Repeating and Working-Through (Further Recommendations on the Technique of Psycho-Analysis II)', in *The Standard Edition of the Complete Psychological Works of Sigmund Freud, Volume XII (1911-1913)* (London: The Hogarth Press and The Institute of Psychoanalysis, 1958), pp. 145-56.

Sigmund Freud (1916), 'Criminals from a Sense of Guilt', in 'Some Character-Types Met with in Psychoanalytic Work', in *The Standard Edition of the Complete Psychological Works of Sigmund Freud, Volume XIV (1914-1916)* (London: The Hogarth Press and The Institute of Psychoanalysis, 1957), pp. 332-3.

Mervin Glasser, 'Some Aspects of the Role of Aggression in the Perversions', in *Sexual Deviation*, I. Rosen (ed.). Second Edition. (Oxford: Oxford University Press, 1979), pp. 278-305.

Amadeo Limentani, 'A Re-evaluation of Acting Out in Relation to Working Through', *International Journal of Psychoanalysis*, 1966, 47:274-82.

Donald Winnicott (1956), 'The Anti-social Tendency', in *The Collected Works of D.W. Winnicott, Volume 5, 1955-1959*, Lesley Caldwell, Helen Taylor Robinson (eds) (Oxford: Oxford University Press, 2017).

Carnal Knowledge: Three Cases

Leo Bersani, *The Freudian Body: Psychoanalysis and Art* (New York: Columbia University Press, 1986).

Judith Butler, *The Psychic Life of Power* (Stanford: Stanford University Press, 1997).

Sigmund Freud (1905), 'Three Essays on the Theory of Sexuality', in *The Standard Edition of the Complete Psychological Works of Sigmund Freud, Volume VII (1901-1905)* (London: The Hogarth Press and The Institute of Psychoanalysis, 1953), pp. 123-246.

Melanie Klein, 'The Oedipus Complex in the Light of Early Anxieties', *International Journal of Psychoanalysis*, 1945, 26:11-32.

Julia Kristeva, *Powers of Horror* (New York: Columbia University Press, 1982).

Adam Limentani, 'To the Limits of Male Heterosexuality: The vagina-man', *Journal of Analytic Psychotherapy and Psychopathology*, 1984, 2: 115–29. This essay is also available in *Between Freud and Klein: The Psychoanalytic Quest for Knowledge and Truth* (London: Free Association Books, 1989).

Adam Phillips, *Winnicott* (London: Penguin Books, 2007). Originally published in 1988, this book remains the best introduction to Donald Winnicott and his thinking.

Donald Winnicott (1945), 'Home Again', in *Deprivation and Delinquency*, Clare Winnicott, Ray Shepherd and Madeleine Davis (eds.) (London: Tavistock Publishing, 1984), p. 47.

Donald Winnicott (written with Clare Britton for Human Relations, 1947), 'Residential Management as Treatment for Difficult Children', in *Deprivation and Delinquency*, Clare Winnicott, Ray Shepherd and Madeleine Davis (eds.) (London, Tavistock Publishing, 1984), p. 52.

Donald Winnicott, 'Hate in the Counter-Transference', *International Journal of Psychoanalysis*, 1949, 30:69–74, also in *Through Paediatrics to Psycho-Analysis* (London: The Hogarth Press, 1982), p. 199.

Connections

The characters and events portrayed in this story, other than those clearly in the public domain, are fictitious and any resemblance to real persons, living or dead, is purely coincidental.

The phrase 'what's good for the pike is death for the minnow' is a paraphrase of 'freedom for the pike is death for the minnows', a quote from *Two Concepts of Liberty*, the inaugural lecture delivered by Isaiah Berlin at the University of Oxford on 31 October 1958. *Two Concepts of Liberty* (Oxford: Oxford University Press, 1958), p. 9.

The phrase 'take what you want, and pay for it' comes from the Spanish saying: '*Y Dios le dijo al hombre: "Toma lo que deseas, y paga por ello."*' 'And God said to man: "Take what you want, and pay for it."'

The quote from the psychoanalyst Wilfred Bion was originally reported in Robert Gosling, 'Gosling on Bion', *The Tavistock Gazette*, Diamond Jubilee Issue, 1980, pp. 22–3. It is quoted in N. Symington, *The Analytic Experience: Lectures from the Tavistock* (London: Free Association Books, 1986), p. 278, and also N. Symington, 'Where is the medicine of healing in psychoanalysis?', *Australasian Journal of Psychotherapy*, 2005, 25:2, 6–22.

Roland Barthes, *The Lover's Discourse*, translated by Richard Howard (New York: Hill and Wang, 1978). See: Section 4 in 'Dark Glasses', p. 43.

Francis Grier (ed.), *Oedipus and the Couple* (London: Karnac Books, 2005; reprinted London: Routledge, 2019).

Mary Morgan, 'On Being Able to be a Couple: The importance of a "creative couple" in psychic life', in *Oedipus and the Couple*, Francis Grier (ed.) (London: Karnac Books, 2005), pp. 9–30.

Mary Morgan, *A Couple State of Mind: Psychoanalysis of Couples and the Tavistock Relationships Model* (London: Routledge, 2019).

The Gift

Iris Murdoch, 'The Sublime and the Good', in *Existentialists and Mystics, Writings on Philosophy and Literature*, Peter Conradi (ed.) (New York: The Penguin Press, 1998), pp. 205–20.

Sparks

Dr Marie Battle Singer was the first Black psychoanalyst in Britain. For more information about her remarkable life, see: Jane Rhodes and

Lynn Hudson, *From Mississippi to Cambridge: Marie Battle Singer, Britain's first Black psychoanalyst* (Wolfson Hall, Cambridge, 2021), https://vimeo.com/522837361.

Ann Bolt, 'In Memoriam Marie Battle Singer', *Journal of Child Psychotherapy*, 1985, 11 (2):3.

Janet Malcolm, *Reading Chekhov: A critical journey* (London: Granta Books, 2001).

James Burns Singer, *Collected Poems*, edited with an introduction by James Keery (Manchester: Carcanet Press Limited, 2001).

Tomas Tranströmer, 'Track' from *The Half-Finished Heaven: Selected Poems*, translated by Robert Bly (London: Penguin Classics, 2017). Copyright © Tomas Tranströmer and the Estate of Tomas Tranströmer, 2001, 2017. Translation copyright © Robert Bly 2001, 2017. Reprinted by permission of Penguin Books Ltd. in the UK, and in the US and Canada reprinted with the permission of The Permissions Company, LLC on behalf of Graywolf Press, graywolfpress.org.

Love and Time

Sigmund Freud (1916) 'On Transience', *The Standard Edition of the Complete Psychological Works of Sigmund Freud, Volume XIV (1914–1916)* (London: The Hogarth Press and The Institute of Psychoanalysis, 1957), pp. 303–7.

Iris Murdoch, 'The Sovereignty of Good over Other Concepts', in *Existentialism and Mystics, Writings on Philosophy and Literature* by Peter Conradi (ed.) (London: Penguin Books, 1999). In this essay she writes: 'The acceptance of death is an acceptance of our own nothingness which is an automatic spur to our concern with what is not ourself', p. 385. Echoing this sentiment, see Li-Young Lee's beautiful poem 'To Hold', in *Behind My Eyes* (New York: Norton, 2008), p. 98.

SOURCES AND NOTES

Helen Vendler, *Last Looks, Last Books: Stevens, Plath, Lowell, Bishop, Merrill* (Princeton: Princeton University Press, 2010). In her illuminating study, she coins the phrase 'binocular style' to describe looking at both our life and our death.

James Robertson, *A Two-year-old Goes to Hospital*, 16 mm film, 40-minute and 30-minute versions, in English and French (Concord Video and Film Council, 1952). The psychoanalyst James Robertson's pioneering documentary film portrays the enduring emotional damage done by well-meaning doctors and nurses to a child who is too young to understand her surgery or the absence of her mother.

Donald Winnicott, 'Metapsychological and Clinical Aspects of Regression within the Psychoanalytic Set-up', in *Through Paediatrics to Psychoanalysis* (London: The Hogarth Press Ltd, 1958), pp. 278–94.

Going Home

Anton Chekhov (1890), 'Gusev', in *The Witch and Other Stories, Volume VI, The Tales of Anton Chekhov,* translated by Constance Garnett (New York: HarperCollins Books, 1998).

Francine Prose, 'Learning from Chekhov', in *Reading Like a Writer* (New York: Harper Perennial, 2007), pp. 233–48.

James Wood, 'What Chekhov Meant by Life', in *The Broken Estate* (New York: Random House, 2000), pp. 79–90.

Hauntings

Margaret Atwood, 'Descent: Negotiating with the Dead, Who makes the trip to the Underworld, and why?', in *Negotiating with the Dead: A Writer on Writing* (London: Virago, 2003), pp. 137–61.

Christopher Bollas, *The Shadow of the Object: Psychoanalysis of the Unthought Known* (New York: Columbia University Press, 1987).

SOURCES AND NOTES

Donald Campbell and Rob Hale, *Working in the Dark: Understanding the Pre-suicide State of Mind* (London: Routledge, 2017). Modest and profound, the best book I know on the pre-suicidal state of mind and the psychotherapy of the suicidal patient.

André Green, 'The Dead Mother', in *On Private Madness* (London: The Hogarth Press, 1986), pp. 142–73.

Robert Pogue Harrison, *The Dominion of the Dead* (Chicago: University of Chicago Press, 2003).

Robert Macfarlane, *Underland: A Deep Time Journey* (London: Penguin Random House, 2019).

Janet Malcolm, *The Silent Woman: Sylvia Plath and Ted Hughes* (New York: Picador, 1993).

D. Owens, J. Horrocks, and A. House, 'Fatal and Non-fatal Repetition of Self-harm: Systematic review', *British Journal of Psychiatry*, 2002, 181: 193–9.

Adrienne Rich, 'Diving into the Wreck', in *Diving into the Wreck: Poems 1971–1972* (New York: W. W. Norton & Company, Inc., 1973), pp. 22–4.

Rainer Maria Rilke, 'The First Elegy', in *The Poetry of Rilke*, Bilingual Edition, translated by Edward Snow (New York: North Point Press, a Division of Farrar, Straus and Giroux, 2009), pp. 282–9.

Andrew Solomon, *The Noonday Demon: An Atlas of Depression* (London: Vintage, 2002).

Acknowledgements

'Fear is the enemy of writing,' my friend John Lahr says. He and Carin Besser have been my first readers. They both have a feel for words and for storytelling. Their care and acumen have provided a safety net which has given me the freedom to write and to say what I wanted to say. Their discussions about the work have been one of the great pleasures of my life.

This is my second collaboration with Clara Farmer at Chatto & Windus. She knows me well. Clara's understanding, enthusiasm and elegant editing are stamped everywhere into these pages.

An extraordinary group of transatlantic editors have supported this project and polished my prose: at Random House in America, the late, beloved Susan Kamil; Andy Ward who took on this book with energy and enthusiasm. I am grateful also for the careful reading and advice of Hilary Redmon at Random House, and Sarah St. Pierre at Random House Canada.

In this roll-call of gratitude, bravos also to the team of publicity, marketing and design talent who have helped to launch the book so well. In London, for Chatto & Windus/Vintage: Priya

ACKNOWLEDGEMENTS

Roy, Fergus Edmondson and Kris Potter. Thanks also to managing editor Graeme Hall, copy editor Alison Tulett and assistant editor Rosanna Hildyard – they made this book better. In New York, at Random House: Carrie Neill, Ayelet Durantt, Julia Harrison and Alison Rich.

Georgia Garrett, who I am lucky to call my agent, gave me insightful notes. A salute, too, to all the wonderful people at Rogers, Coleridge & White, especially Sam Coates, Stephen Edwards, Tristan Kendrick, Laurence Laluyaux, Ivy Pottinger-Glass and Peter Straus. In New York, my continuing thanks to Melanie Jackson.

In *Love's Labour*'s slow progress to completion, many people were kind enough to read drafts: Catrin Aaronovitch, David Aaronovitch, Christopher Bollas, Susanne Calice, Donald Campbell, Clare Carlisle, Wendy Cope, Adam Duncan, Anjali Grier, Francis Grier, Lynn Hudson, Cornelia von Kleist, Stephen Lehmann, Paul Mayersberg, Carl Miller, Anna Monk, Masaaki Nishimura, Alejandra Perez, Penny Pilzer, whom I miss, Siân Putnam, Jane Rhodes, Julia Samuel, John Scholar, Jonathan Sheldon, Ben Stambler, Helen Tyson and Bettina von Zwehl. And for their notes of various drafts and the final manuscript, a shout-out to my friends Mark Ellingham, Robert Icke, Natania Jansz and Zara Tempest-Walters.

I wish I wrote books faster, so I could more often enjoy the pleasure of publicly thanking my wife, Nicola Luckhurst. From the outset of our relationship twenty-five years ago, the ideas in

Love's Labour have been a part of our conversation. An astute reader with a deep knowledge of literature, I am fortunate to have her read my stories and share her understanding. I am grateful to her for this, and so very much more. I dedicate this book to Nicola and our beloved and loving children.

Finally, I want to thank the group of people I cannot thank by name: my patients.

About the Author

Stephen Grosz is a practising psychoanalyst – he has worked with patients for more than forty years. Born in America, he was educated at the University of California, Berkeley, and at the University of Oxford, and now lives in London. His number one *Sunday Times* bestseller *The Examined Life* has been translated into more than thirty languages.